More Furniture in 24 Hours

More Furniture in 24 Hours

Spiros Zakas

and his students
at Parsons School of Design

Photographs by
Marc Raboy

ST. MARTIN'S PRESS   NEW YORK

To Peter Zakas, my brother,
and Bern Conrad, my good friend

Library of Congress Cataloging in Publication Data

Zakas, Spiros.
    More furniture in 24 hours.

    1. Furniture making—Amateurs' manuals.
I. Parsons School of Design, New York.   II. Title.
TT195.Z35   684.1   78-3989
ISBN 0-312-54803-6
ISBN 0-312-54804-4 pbk.

Contents

Preface

Since publishing the first book of *Furniture in 24 Hours,* I have received an astonishing number of letters from people who have used—and, in many cases, further developed—our designs, people of all ages and various countries who are delighted to be making things with their heads and with their hands. It's been wonderfully rewarding to see people expressing such interest in creating furniture for their homes and for their family and friends to share. This is especially heartening in a country like the United States where commercialism is probably at its strongest pitch, relentlessly urging on us a vast array of prefabricated items that constitute the lifeblood of a consumers' society.

Today television encourages us to buy freeze-dried coffee instead of grinding those coffee beans ourselves. You don't even need to peel a potato any longer: they come frozen in puffs, strings, mashed, and soufflé. That most basic of foods, the egg, is now available already scrambled in a carton; if you don't want to mess up a pan, you can get them frozen, just warm and serve. And should the effort of heating an egg become disturbing, you can always go to McDonald's for an egg McMuffin.

Or you can make yourself a simple omelette: cheaper, more elegant, seasoned to your own taste. It's easy. And you have the pleasure of doing it yourself. We forget that doing it *is* a pleasure.

I've always been interested in the pleasures of doing.

This is a book about making furniture and making choices. You can spend all you can afford—and often more than you can afford—on preprocessed, prepackaged furniture. You often see young couples spending thousands of dollars they can ill afford furnishing one living room. Or you can make yourself a chair in five hours for $11; or an elegant dining room table in eight hours for $30.

What makes this possible is today's technology. At the Parsons School of Design, where I teach, our students spend time studying different periods of history and design. We see how the Orient uses bamboo, rattan, and reeds, and how plastics have changed Italian and American design. We observe how the classic styles of the age of Napoleon, or Louis XV, or Queen Anne influence contemporary designs. We learn that politics and climates, materials and technology, have created the great design styles of the past. And we use today's tools and materials to design for the present.

There is, for example, an exciting variety of new materials. Chipboard is made of particles of wood that have been glued together. Masonite is a form of chipboard that has been tempered so it's smooth, nonporous, and flexible. Both are strong, easily worked with, and readily available. Hollowcore doors are made of two wood veneers glued together with a honeycomb sandwich construction; they can be used to make a classically simple folding screen or an elegant lounge chair. Gypsum board, a byproduct of recycled paper, is another new resource. We even use honeycomb cardboard, so strong movers use it for pallets on loading docks. And Urethane foam makes it possible to upholster this furniture quickly and elegantly.

We can take advantage of new, inexpensive, and portable tools for cutting, sanding, and drilling. We now have that completely marvelous tool, the staple gun. But the biggest advance in tools in the past fifteen years has been in glues. We now have bonding as easy to use as Elmer's glue and stronger than the bonded material itself.

Just as important as the development of new tools and materials are the novel social conditions we find ourselves living in, especially the increased mobility of our lives and therefore of our dwellings. Years ago people bought furniture as they did houses—for life. Today these large, heavy expensive pieces seemed designed to fix life forever in a single set of choices with no possibility for growth or innovation. But today we are constantly moving, to larger or smaller spaces, or to different sections of the country, according to our needs. Our lives change. We are on a journey—and we may wish to travel light. We are less interested in permanent possessions than in continuities of value and experience.

These new possibilities and circumstances will not give us the designs of the past. But they can give rise to, and make available to all, styles which are just as attractive and elegant. Take mobility, for example: the superb tents and tee-pees of nomadic Arabs and American Plains Indians show that mobility need not hinder good design, design which is cleaner and more refined as it more openly expresses its materials and functions.

You probably don't live in a tent. What you want is not the forms of the great styles of the past, but rather their clarity, utility, and beauty. One of the best ways to get these qualities is to make your own furniture. We value antiques largely for their loving craftsmanship. The new technology makes the pleasures of craftsmanship available to everyone. Making things is an art, whether it's baking bread, sewing a quilt, or building a table. It is self-expression, a way of knowing what we like and how we like it, of discovering who we are. The interesting thing I have found is that everyone is creative in many ways if he or she will only try them. Just because you have never done something doesn't mean that you can't. And there is no better place to start than in your home. Make it *yours* with objects you have made to suit yourself and to share with friends. And don't feel you must live with something you make forever. Pass it on to a friend who has appreciated it; it will always be special.

The design recipes in this book will not only give you the experience of making things yourself. They will give you the bright individuality, the outspoken quality, that handmade-to-order objects impart. Any chair, after all, is essentially a back and a seat, but those requirements can be met in a variety of ways, some much more interesting and original than anything you can find in stores. The designs here, by my students and myself, have style and humor and a love of materials, simplicity, and expression. But they aren't meant to limit you. Add a cushion. Lacquer a piece that we painted. Adapt our thoughts to suit your own convenience and imagination. Or invent something new.

This book is meant to be practical. But the most practical thing in the world is to change your philosophy, your attitude, how you see things, how you do things, what you want, what the possibilities are. The various pieces in this book are meant to open up your mind, or to reinforce that openness to show you what's possible, what's fun, and what can be deeply satisfying as well as comfortable, elegant, and cheap. Life is what you make it, even today; your home is what you make it, especially today; and furniture can be what you make it, starting today.

Space
Bench

George Thomopoulos

Cost: $19 Time: 4 hours

Materials

— one piece plywood, interior finish, 48"
x 96" x ¾"
— white glue
— nails
— stain or paint (optional)

Tools

— jigsaw
— hammer
— sandpaper

Method

Examine illustrations
— cut plywood into two equal pieces,
each measuring 48" x 48"
— on one piece draw a diagonal and cut
it with the jigsaw
— on the other piece, measure 10" from
two opposite corners towards one of

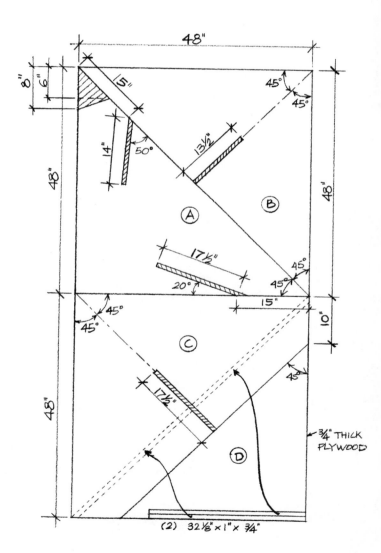

the other two other opposite ones (see diagram)

— draw a line connecting the two points, and cut the piece off; put the small piece aside

— the two equal pieces are numbered A and B; C will be the larger piece

— according to Diagram ● we draw and then cut off two ridges of piece A

— diagram ● ● shows us how we cut off one ridge

— the diagram ● ● ● shows what we do with piece C: first make a ridge here, then draw a line connecting the two opposite corners; right under the line nail two strips that were cut off the piece put aside

— first slide the piece C into piece A from the back (standing position) till it hits the floor

— the B piece is pushed into the other ridge on piece A until it touches piece C and rests on the two strips added to piece C

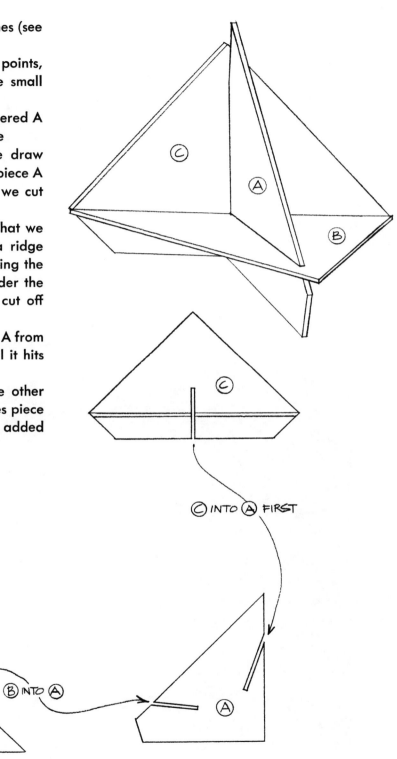

Ⓒ INTO Ⓐ FIRST

Ⓑ INTO Ⓐ

V
Armchair

Yutaka Matsumoto

Cost: $11 Time: 5 hours (the first time)

Materials

— one piece plywood, ¾" x 4' x 4'
— one pint gloss enamel paint

Tools

— electric saw
— sandpaper
— brush

Method

Examine illustrations
— cut plywood into four pieces
— cut out slots (¾" wide) on each piece; be careful with angle

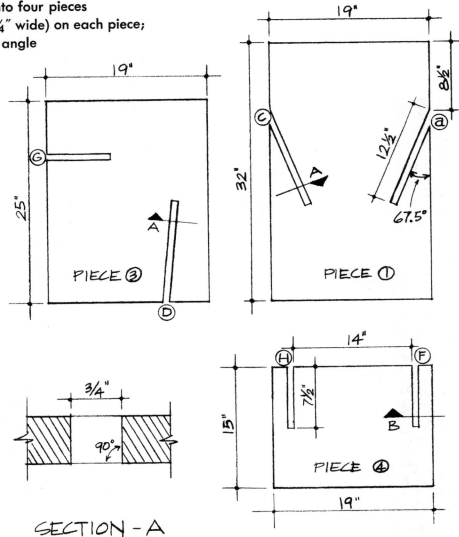

SECTION - A

- assemble pieces 1 and 2 with slots a and b
- assemble pieces 1 and 3 with slots c and d
- assemble pieces 4 and 2, and 3 with slots e and f, g and h
- sand all surfaces and soften the top edge of piece 1
- paint

Note: for barstool, lounge chair, or coffee table, same method to be used. See sketch drawing.

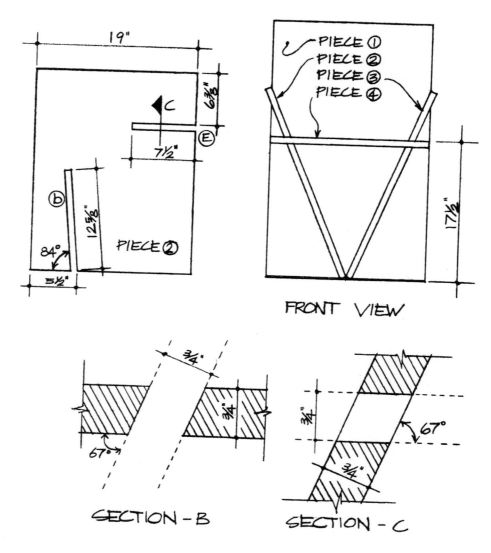

FRONT VIEW

SECTION – B

SECTION – C

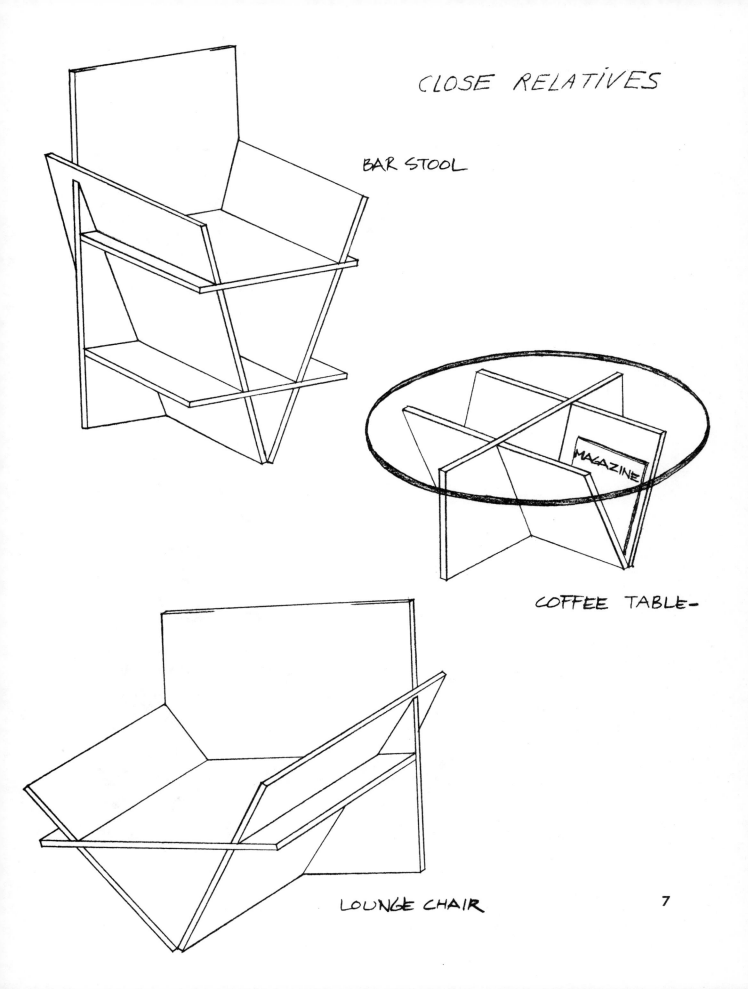

CLOSE RELATIVES

BAR STOOL

COFFEE TABLE

MAGAZINE

LOUNGE CHAIR

7

The
W Chair

by Daniel J. Cohen

Cost: $26 Time: 8 hours

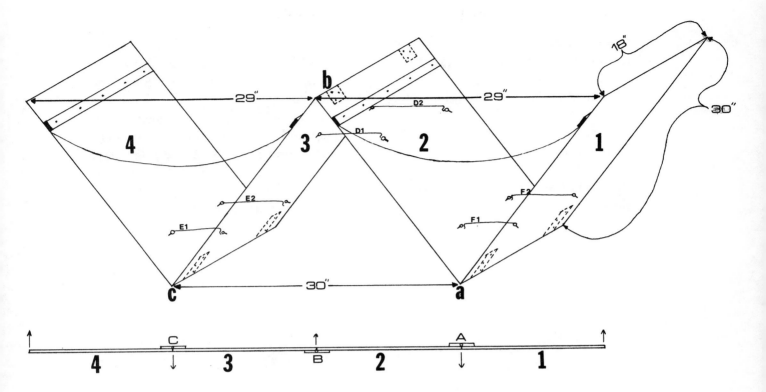

Materials

— four pieces of ¾" plywood, each 18" x 30"
— six hinges, 4" x 4"
— six 12"-long latches with screw eyes
— 2 yds. very heavy canvas
— four pieces of hardwood stripping, each ⅜" x 1" x 18"
— one box wood screws ⅝", ¼" thread
— twenty 1" sheet metal screws, ¼" thread with ¾" diameter washers
— ⅜" staples for gun

Tools

— electric drill
— drill bits: ⅛", 3⁄16", ¼"
— screwdriver
— staple gun
— tape measure
— sandpaper, fine and medium
— 4" C-clamps
— 12" hacksaw
— file

Method

Examine illustrations
— sand all pieces with medium and then with fine sandpaper
— line up all four pieces of wood and lay out hinges connecting pieces 1 and 2, 3 and 4; position hinge 2" in from each side and mark the holes
— select 3⁄16" bit and drill all the holes
— attach the hinges
— repeat the process, connecting 2 and 3; put these hinges on the reverse side
— pull point B up till A and C are 30" apart, as shown in diagram

9

— screw in two eye hooks, as shown in drawings, 3" from the D1 and D2
— do the same connecting E1 and E2, F1 and F2 (important: these should be 29" apart)
— cut two pieces of canvas 18" x 33" (finished size)
— staple the canvas to the hardwood strips and fold over till staples do not show

— clamp the strips to the plywood with the C-clamps in the desired position, approximately 18" from the floor; center
— using ⅛" bit, drill five holes evenly spaced through the canvas-wood strip and plywood; be sure to attach sheet metal screws and washers to the wood
— now fold the chair up!

Lockdown Coffee Table

George Thomopoulos

Cost: $9 Time: 4 hours

Materials

—— one piece of birch plywood 48" x 30"
x ¾"
—— white glue
—— 1" nails
—— plastic wood

Tools

—— electric saw
—— jigsaw
—— hammer
—— sander

Method

Examine illustrations
—— from the plywood, cut off four ½" x
¾" strips from outer perimeter
—— as per diagram, measure 3½" from the sides of remaining piece; cut out the middle piece, being careful to follow diagram
—— divide the 3½" x 48" x 30" piece into four equal parts (shaded parts are waste)
—— take parts A, B, C, D and make a ridge 2" x ¾" on the place shown by diagram ● ● ●
—— diagram ● ● shows how the four strips ½" x ¾" are divided and placed on underside of top piece E
—— diagram ● ● ● ● shows how legs interlock in one direction
—— diagram ● ● ● ● ● shows finished product

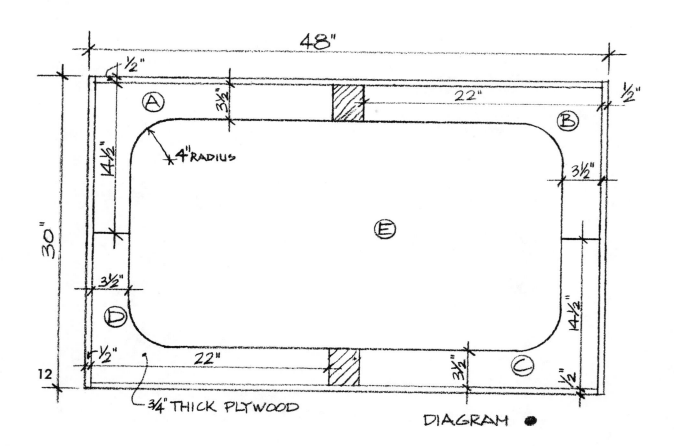

DIAGRAM ●

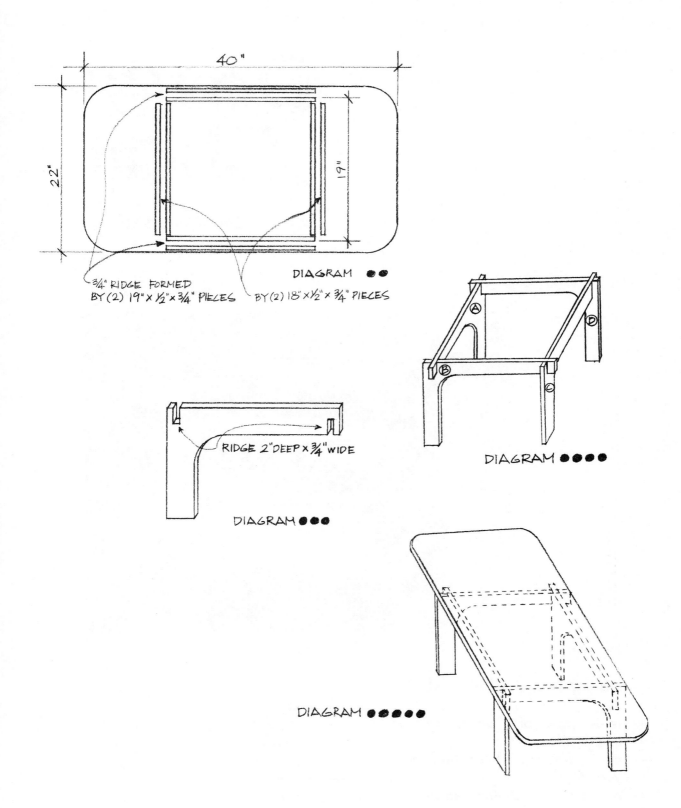

40"

22"

19"

3/4" RIDGE FORMED
BY (2) 19" x 1/2" x 3/4" PIECES

BY (2) 18" x 1/2" x 3/4" PIECES

DIAGRAM ●●

RIDGE 2" DEEP x 3/4" WIDE

DIAGRAM ●●●

DIAGRAM ●●●●

DIAGRAM ●●●●●

13

Dowel Chair

by Michael Rait

Cost: $65 Time: 5 hours

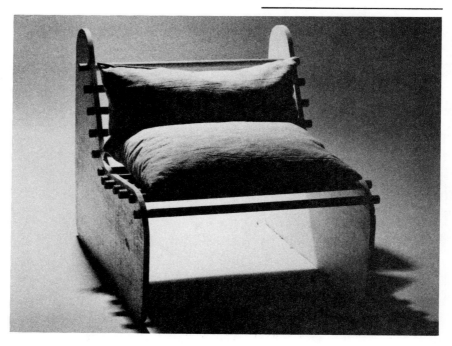

Materials

—— one half-sheet of ¾" plywood, 48" x 48"
—— twelve pieces of 1" dowels, each 36" long
—— one quart wood finish (i.e.: paint, varnish)
—— one large understuffed cushion

Tools

—— jigsaw
—— drill
—— sandpaper
—— paintbrush
—— tape measure
—— compass
—— rubber mallet

Method

Examine illustrations
— cut plywood into two equal sides, as per photo
— drill holes for dowels, all the same distance from the edge, and equally proceed along seat and back of chair (the holes should be made so that the 1" dowels will fit snugly when hammered in with a rubber mallet)
— sand all rough edges and surfaces
— hammer in dowels (leave about 2" sticking out on either side of chair)
— place cushion on seat

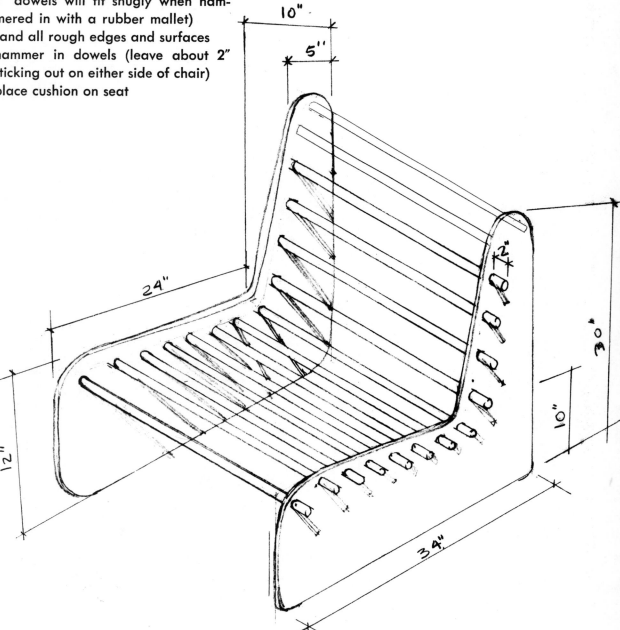

Tarantula Chandelier

Karen L. Simon

Cost: $30 Time: 3 hours

Materials
—— eight white Christmas lights
—— string of Christmas light sockets
—— 12' sculpture wire
—— 1 yd. of black fur, 36" wide
—— ⅓ yd. of black vinyl, 36" wide
—— 1 square foot of foam rubber
—— piece of plywood ¼" x 12" x 12"
—— hollow steel rod 9" x ⅜" (found in electrical supply store)
—— 18' electrical cord
—— plug
—— electrical tape
—— black enamel paint (small jar)
—— black enamel spray paint
—— two electrical caps

Tools

—— staple gun
—— wire cutter
—— drill
—— scissors
—— sewing machine (or needle and thread)
—— coping saw

Method

Examine illustrations
—— spray the string of sockets black, being careful not to get paint on the inside as that will spoil the electrical connection; spray the steel rod black as well
—— cut the plywood into a circle 9" in diameter and drill a ⅜" hole in center
—— draw a concentric circle with a 7" diameter on the plywood

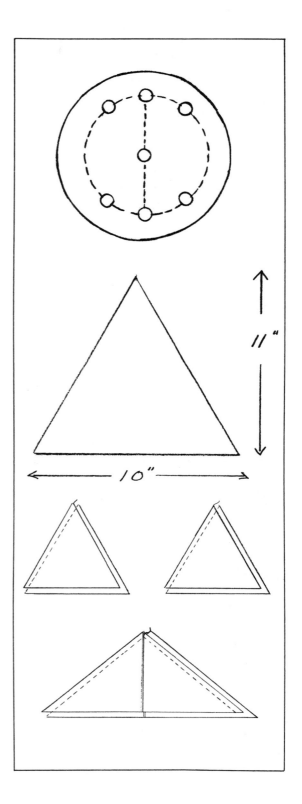

17

- draw the diameter of this circle
- where the diameter meets the 7" circle, drill a ⅜" hole at each intersection
- 2" either side of each hole, along the circumference of the 7" circle drill a ⅜" hole (you will have just drilled seven holes in total)
- cut six 20" pieces of sculpture wire and two 12" pieces and put aside

Body

- cut four pieces of fur fabric in triangle shapes measuring 10" at the base and 11" in height
- place one triangle on another, right sides matching, and sew one seam down the side ½" from the edge
- take the next two triangles and repeat the procedure
- now match the two sets of triangles right side to right side, and sew seams down both edges (making sure to leave ½" at edge)
- turn this whole piece inside out, and you will have a dome-shaped body structure

Legs

- cut six pieces of fur material 3½" by 18"
- fold one piece in half lengthwise so that the right sides are matching
- sew a seam down that side ¼" from the edge
- repeat this procedure with remaining five legs
- since this is a narrow piece, it is diffi-

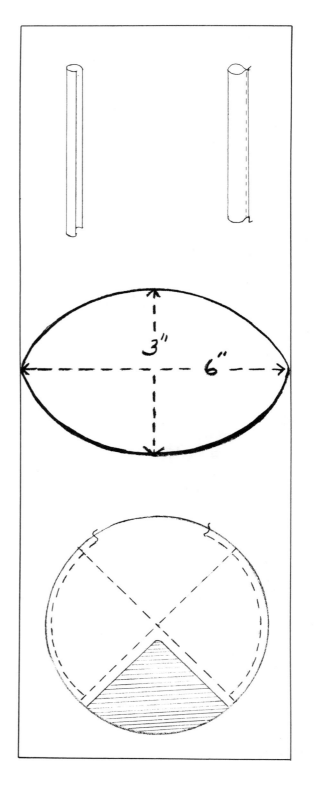

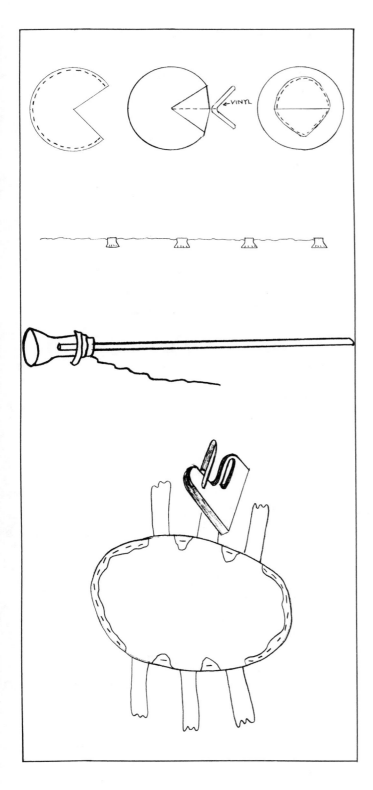

cult to turn inside out; fold out the top so that it forms a rim around the rest of the piece and push the rest of the piece up through, pulling down on the rim at the same time to release more fabric (your 9" rod will be very useful in pushing the fabric through)

Head

— cut two circles out of the fur with a 7" diameter and one oval of vinyl fabric measuring 6" at longest point and 3" across

— on the wrong side, draw the diameter on one circle, then draw another diameter, perpendicular to the first

— inside one triangle draw two lines, ½" from each radius

— place this circle on top of other circle, right sides matching, and cut out the triangle you've drawn

— sew a seam ½" from circumference, leaving the triangular area and a 3" area opposite triangular area unsewn

— take the piece of vinyl and match it to triangular opening, right side to right side, and pin it all the way around

— sew a seam all around the "mouthpiece" ½" from edge

— turn head inside out

Electrical

— clip the wire very close to the socket on one side and very close to the next socket on the other side (usually the sockets are interspersed every 12" along the cord)

— take one 20" piece of sculpture wire and, using the electrical tape, tape

the wire to the socket, making sure that the tape covers the small piece of exposed electrical cord
— the length of cord that extends from the socket will not be long enough to run through the leg, so you must splice an additional length of cord to it
— bare the ends of the cord (with the wire cutter) and bare the ends of 12" of wire so that the copper is exposed
— twist each together and wrap electrical tape around it
— repeat this procedure with remaining five pieces
— take a length of sculpture wire and one socket (with cord attached) and push it through a fabric leg so that only the tip of the socket extends past the fabric
— repeat this procedure with the remaining five legs
— take the piece of plywood and the "legs" and one by one thread the electrical cord and the "2" of sculpture wire down through the holes
— bend wire so that it lies flat against the underside of the wood
— use the staple gun to fasten sculpture wire to wood
— repeat with remaining five legs
— turn wood over and staple the leg fabric to the wood, being careful not to pierce the wires
— take the 9" rod and insert it into the central hole so that 1" of it protrudes on the underside (the side with all the wires); it should fit snugly
— take the fabric body and put it over the rod, letting the rod come through the hole in the center of the fabric

— thread the rest of the electrical cord through the rod, bringing it through to the bottom; bare the ends of this cord

Eyes

— cut two 1" x's in the head where eyes should be
— take two more sockets and two lengths of sculpture wire 12" long apiece
— use electrical tape and tape a wire to each socket
— thread wire through x's in head so that the lip of the socket sticks out
— take these sculpture wires and staple them to the underside of wood so that the back of the head touches the wood (if the electrical wires are not long enough to reach, splice additional wire to it)
— paint two black dots on two bulbs to form pupils of eye

Finishing Touches

— take one exposed electrical wire from each leg and from each eye, and twist them together with one wire from the central cord
— take the remaining wires and twist them together with the other part of central cord
— put an electrical cap over each, and put tape around any bare wire which is exposed
— now, stuff foam between top side of wood and fabric body until it feels firm
— pull a 1" circumference of the body

fabric to underside of wood, and tack all the way around with a staplegun (if you've stuffed it too full to do this, take out some foam)
— always be careful not to pierce any electrical wires, and where the body fabric meets a leg, just turn the fabric under a little and tack on either side of the leg

— cut out a 12″ circle from vinyl fabric
— before attaching bottom piece of fabric, screw in all bulbs and attach plug to end of cord; plug it in to check all connections
— take fabric and staple it to underside of wood, turning under the rim of the fabric as you go along
— suspend from ceiling, and plug it in

Folding
Stool

John Kellas

Cost: $6 Time: 2 hours

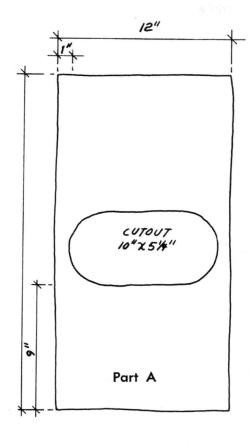

12"

1"

CUTOUT
10" X 5¼"

9"

Part A

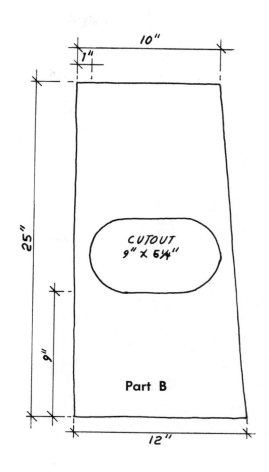

10"

1"

25"

CUTOUT
9" X 5¼"

9"

Part B

12"

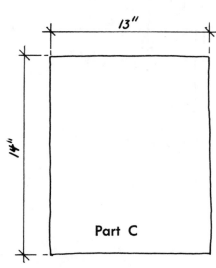

13"

14"

Part C

Materials

— ¾" or ⅝" scrap plywood
— hinges with removable pins
— four hinges

Tools

— jigsaw
— drill with ¼" or larger bit
— handsaw or radial saw
— screwdriver
— nail (to make starter holes for screws)
— compass
— yardstick
— sandpaper
— carpenter's square (optional)

23

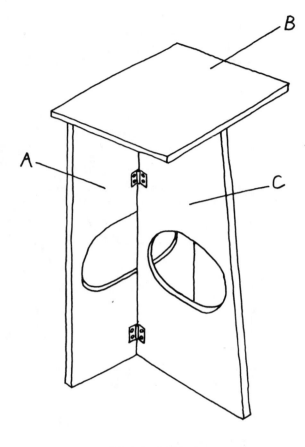

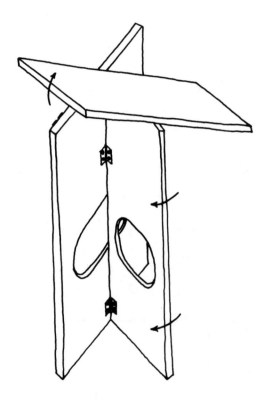

OPEN POSITION

FOLDING METHOD

Method

Examine illustrations
—— cut the parts out of the plywood according to the dimension drawings, using the handsaw or the radial saw
—— sand your plywood smooth
—— with the compass and yardstick, draw the outline of the cutouts on parts A and C
—— drill a starter hole just within each outline

24

- use the jigsaw to cut the shapes out
- lightly sand all edges
- attach the hinges as shown to parts A and C
- attach hinges as shown in seat detail to parts B and C
- attach lock hinge as shown in seat details to front of parts B and A
- to fold, slip pin out of lock hinge and fold as shown

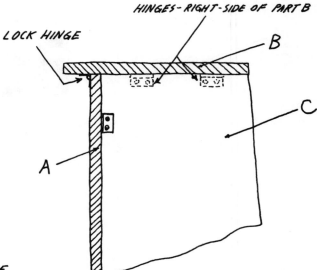

HINGES - RIGHT - SIDE OF PART B

LOCK HINGE

B

C

A

SEAT DETAIL - SIDE VIEW

B

LOCK HINGE

A

SEAT DETAIL - FRONT VIEW

Drawing Storage Bookcase

Daniel Perry

Cost: $9 Time: 5 hours

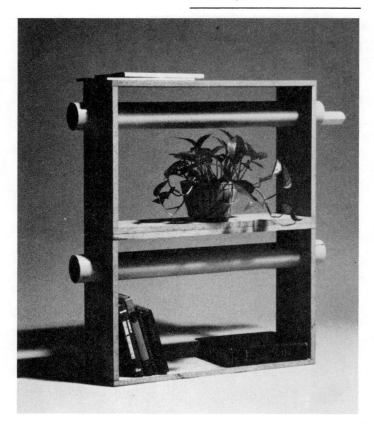

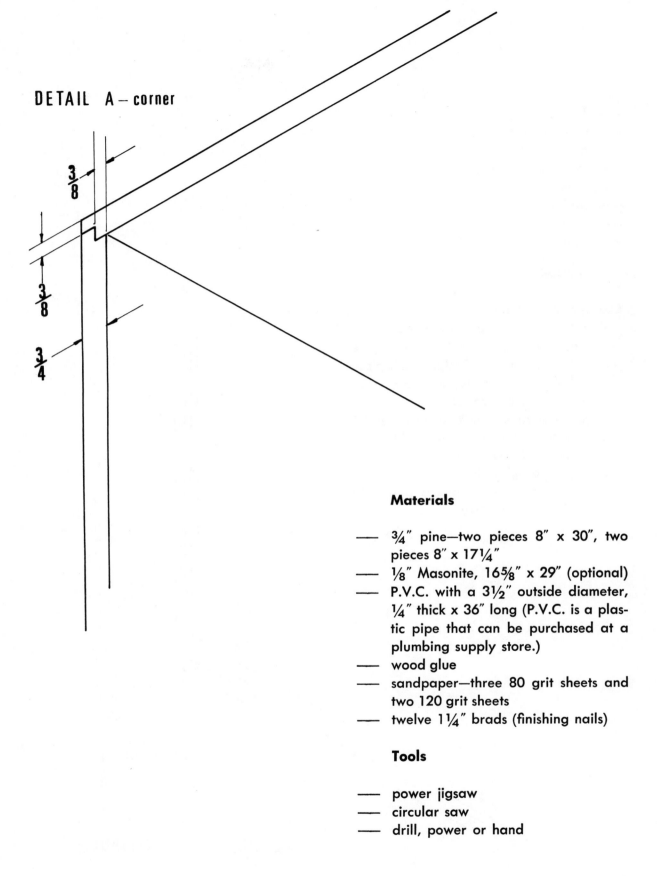

DETAIL A — corner

$\frac{3}{8}$

$\frac{3}{8}$

$\frac{3}{4}$

Materials

— $\frac{3}{4}$" pine—two pieces 8" x 30", two pieces 8" x 17$\frac{1}{4}$"
— $\frac{1}{8}$" Masonite, 16$\frac{5}{8}$" x 29" (optional)
— P.V.C. with a 3$\frac{1}{2}$" outside diameter, $\frac{1}{4}$" thick x 36" long (P.V.C. is a plastic pipe that can be purchased at a plumbing supply store.)
— wood glue
— sandpaper—three 80 grit sheets and two 120 grit sheets
— twelve 1$\frac{1}{4}$" brads (finishing nails)

Tools

— power jigsaw
— circular saw
— drill, power or hand

— ½" bit
— crosscut wood saw
— hacksaw
— four corner clamps
— tape measure
— rubber mallet
— hammer
— compass

Method

Examine illustrations
— cut to size listed under materials
— (see detail A) cut a lap on all pine pieces, along all 8" edges each piece ⅜" wide x ⅜" deep, using a circular saw set to the correct depth with a guide or router, making sure that the side that will face in is the right side
— *OPTIONAL:* on inside edge of back cut a lap ⅛" wide x ¼" deep along entire edge of all pieces (masonite back will fit in there)

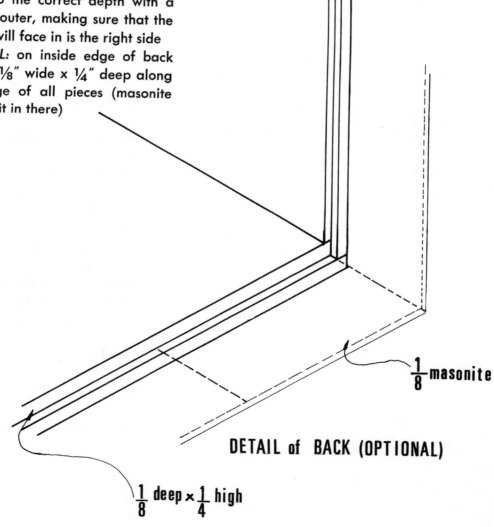

$\frac{1}{8}$ masonite

DETAIL of BACK (OPTIONAL)

$\frac{1}{8}$ deep x $\frac{1}{4}$ high

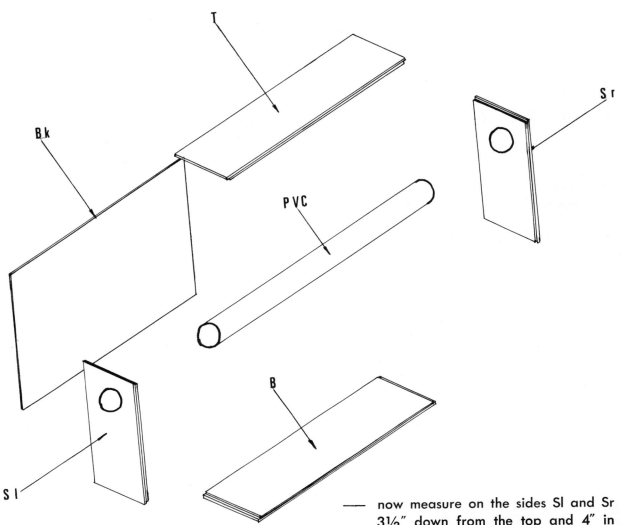

T

Bk

Sr

PVC

Sl

B

— now measure on the sides Sl and Sr 3½" down from the top and 4" in from the other side (this is the center point of the hole to be cut out); take your compass, set it with a 1¾" radius, and draw a circle
— take the drill with ½" bit and drill a hole at the center point of the circle; take jigsaw with the medium blade and "rough cut" the hole, leaving about ¼" around to be taken off with the fine blade; remove remaining ¼"
— sand the hole until the P.V.C. will fit snugly when you tap on it with the rubber mallet; remove the P.V.C. after checking the fit

29

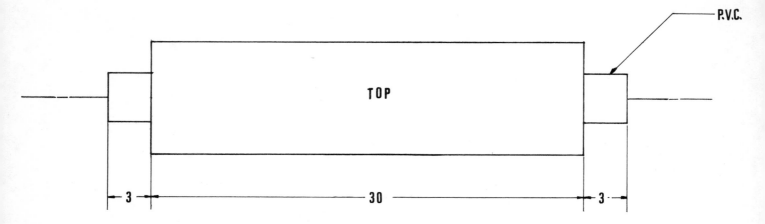

TOP

|— 3 —|———————— 30 ————————|— 3 —|

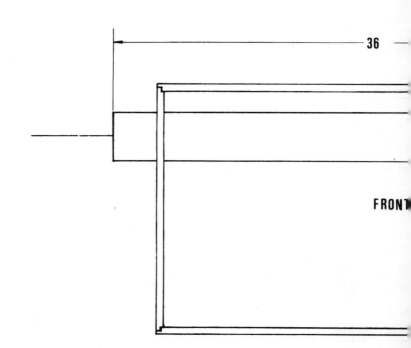

P.V.C.

36

FRONT

— measure from the end 36" at a couple of different points along circumference; this will guide you when you cut

— take the hacksaw and put P.V.C., turning tubing as you cut (this will allow you to cut along all dots, giving a straight cut)

— sand entire pieces with 80 grit sandpaper

— now, take the sides Sl and Sr and tap them 3" on the P.V.C. with the rubber mallet (be sure that the inside is facing in and that the laps for the back are facing back)

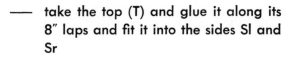

— take the top (T) and glue it along its 8" laps and fit it into the sides Sl and Sr
— clamp the top to the sides using the corner clamps for extra strength
— put three brad into top from the sides
— repeat for bottom
— glue and tack on the back (B)
— light sand with 120 grit sandpaper, and apply finish of your choice

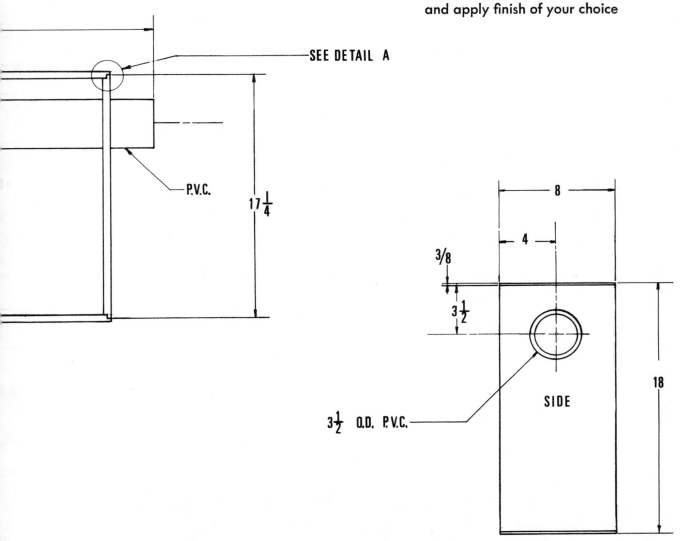

SEE DETAIL A

P.V.C.

$17\frac{1}{4}$

8

4

3/8

$3\frac{1}{2}$

18

SIDE

$3\frac{1}{2}$ O.D. P.V.C.

Gossip
Bench

Mario Locsin

Cost: $10 Time: 4 hours

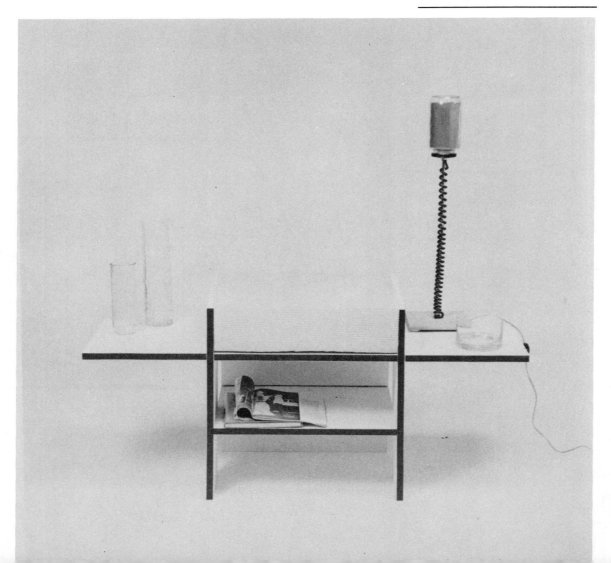

Materials

 ¾" plywood (4' x 4')
— carpenter's glue
— 5" polyurethane foam (18½" x 17")

Tools

— jigsaw
— sandpaper

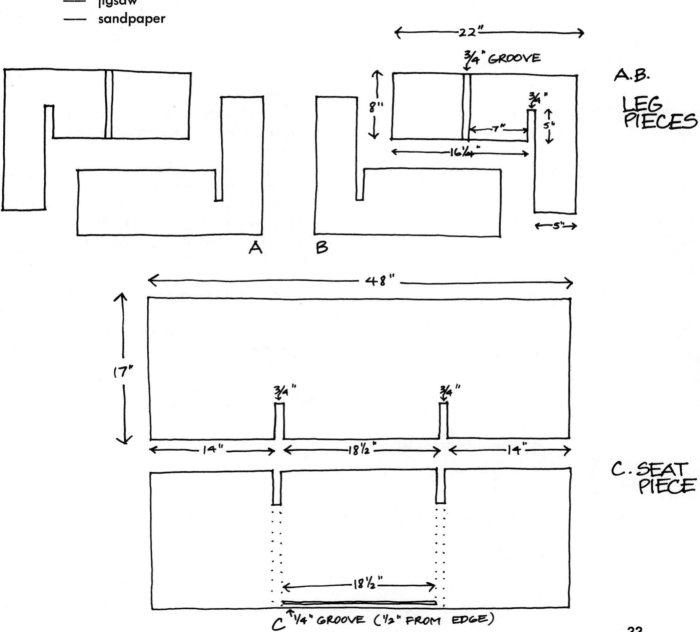

A

B

A.B.
LEG PIECES

C. SEAT PIECE

C ↑¼" GROOVE (½" FROM EDGE)

33

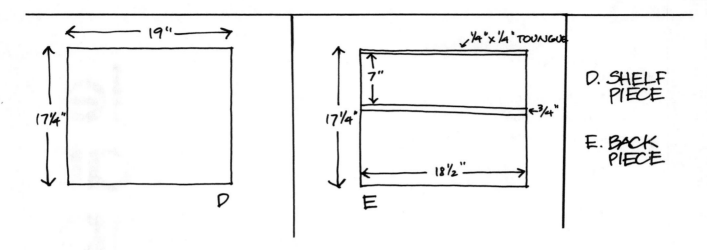

19"

17¼"

D

¼" x ¼" TOUNGUE

7"

17¼"

←¾"

18½"

E

D. SHELF
PIECE

E. BACK
PIECE

Method

Examine illustrations
— cut out all parts, as per drawing (two
  leg pieces, seat piece, shelf piece, and
  back piece)
— cut ¾" grooves (make sure grooves
  are inside on leg pieces)
— make ¼" x ¼" "tongue" on back
  piece (be sure tongue is well cut)
— apply carpenter's glue on all joints
— sand, finish, and assemble
— let dry
— paint, and stripe edges in contrasting
  color
— cover foam with favorite material
— sit and gossip

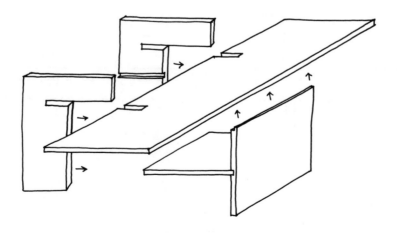

Pickle Jar Lamp

Mario Locsin

Cost: $7 Time: 2 hours

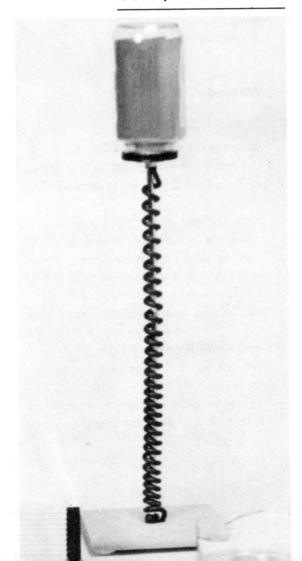

Materials

— ¾" plywood or chopping board
— spray paint
— large pickle jar (B and G)
— bulb
— porcelain socket
— water supply pipe
— coil or telephone wire
— drill for hole or other means
— plug
— switch
— four wooden stands
— threading for pipe in hardware or other means

Tools

— wood saw
— screwdriver
— mat knife

Method

Examine illustrations
— prepare all materials
— cut small opening on jar cap with mat knife, about 1" diameter smaller than socket
— spray-paint
— assemble wiring on metal back to positive and negative screws
— sandwich jar cap between socket and back with wire attached; put aside
— cut hole on square wooden base (center)
— make sure pipe fits in tight
— cut another hole (smaller) on its side for wire
— assemble pipe through hole, and attach switch plate underneath securely

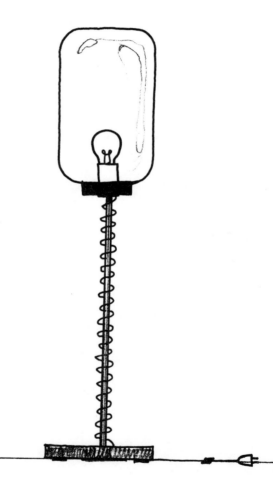

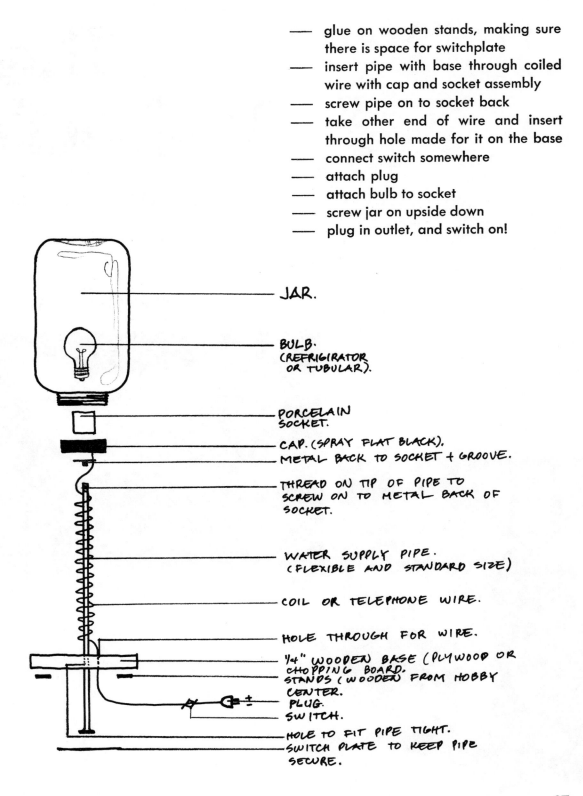

— glue on wooden stands, making sure there is space for switchplate
— insert pipe with base through coiled wire with cap and socket assembly
— screw pipe on to socket back
— take other end of wire and insert through hole made for it on the base
— connect switch somewhere
— attach plug
— attach bulb to socket
— screw jar on upside down
— plug in outlet, and switch on!

JAR.

BULB.
(REFRIGIRATOR
OR TUBULAR).

PORCELAIN
SOCKET.

CAP. (SPRAY FLAT BLACK).
METAL BACK TO SOCKET + GROOVE.

THREAD ON TIP OF PIPE TO
SCREW ON TO METAL BACK OF
SOCKET.

WATER SUPPLY PIPE.
(FLEXIBLE AND STANDARD SIZE)

COIL OR TELEPHONE WIRE.

HOLE THROUGH FOR WIRE.

1/4" WOODEN BASE (PLYWOOD OR
CHOPPING BOARD.
STANDS (WOODEN FROM HOBBY
CENTER.
PLUG.
SWITCH.

HOLE TO FIT PIPE TIGHT.
SWITCH PLATE TO KEEP PIPE
SECURE.

The
V Chair

Daniel J. Cohen

Cost: $13 Time: 5 hours

Materials

— two pieces ¾" plywood, each 24" x 36"
— one piece ¾" plywood 24" x 15", cut into two triangles
— three 12" eye hooks
— five screw eyes
— six 4" x 4" hinges
— ½" staples
— one box of wood screws, ⅝" flat head

Tools

— electric drill
— assorted drill bits
— screwdriver
— staple gun (heavy duty)
— tape measure
— sandpaper
— hacksaw
— scissors
— razor blades
— file

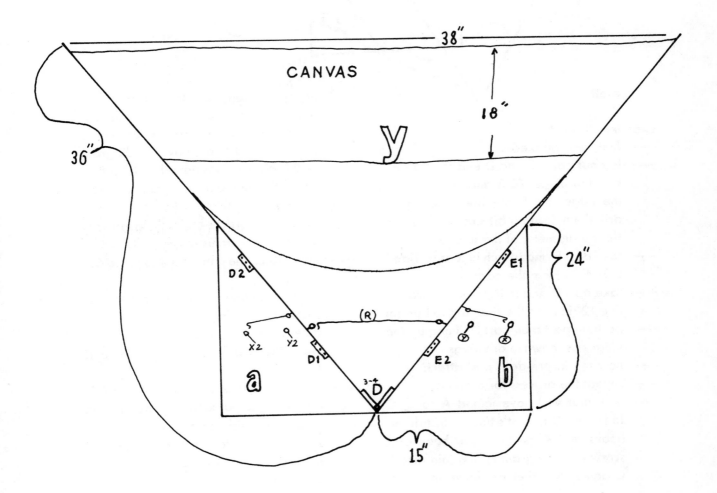

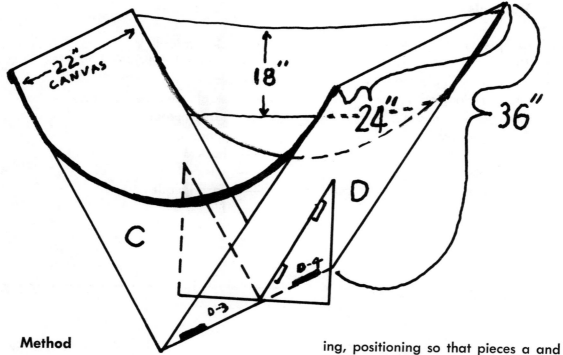

Method

Examine illustrations

— first sand all pieces

— lay out parts C and D end to end and position hinges (D 3 and D 4) 3" from the edge; mark the holes, and pre-drill them, using a bit smaller than the thread diameter of the screws

— take part b and attach hinges (E 1 and E 2) 4" in from the edge

— take part D and in light pencil draw a line 12" in from the side, top to bottom

— position part b on part D, lining up the hinges as shown in drawings

— now mark, pre-drill, and attach

— repeat the process for a and c

— now that you have joined A to C, C to D, and D to B, it's time to install the hooks and eyes: take one hook and screw eye (diagram r) and join pieces C and D together as shown in draw-ing, positioning so that pieces a and b are flat on floor; then install one hook and two screw eyes, attaching pieces A and C as shown in diagram (X 2 should be positioned to keep flap open; Y 2 should be positioned to keep the flap closed)

— repeat the process, attaching parts D and b in the same way

— now attach the canvas; cut a piece 65" x 22"

— now staple one side over the edge, as shown in drawing

— determine the amount of sag you want, then staple to the other side and trim

— attach the back of canvas 40" x 36" by folding to 40" x 18" and positioning as shown in diagrams

— staple it very taut along the outside edge of parts C and D, and then trim as necessary

A Table for Six, to Go

Katherine Pearson

Cost: $30 Time: 8 hours

Materials

— one 36" birch hollowcore door
— one 30" birch hollowcore door
(a polyurethane finish will be more durable than paint on this table, which will be moved about; however, if the table is finished in natural polyurethane, birch doors are recommended over luan)
— two reinforcing wood braces (1¼" x 2" x 36")
— four reinforcing wood braces (1¼" x 2" x 30")
— carpenter's glue
— clear polyurethane varnish
— one 36" x 1½" piano hinge
— two 30" x 1½" piano hinges
— two brass hooks and eyes (3")
— two brass hooks and eyes (2")
— three leather handles (8" x 1¼")
— twelve brass washers
— twelve brass wood screws (¾")

Tools

— tape measure
— pencil
— C-clamps
— medium and fine sandpaper
— brush
— drill or awl
— Phillips-head screwdriver
— chisel and mallet
— standard blade screwdriver

Method

Examine illustrations
— make two cuts in 36" wide door, each cut 30" from the finished ends of the door (these two pieces will be the folding top)
— make two cuts in 30" door, each cut 17¼" from the finished ends of the door, for hinged wings of the table base

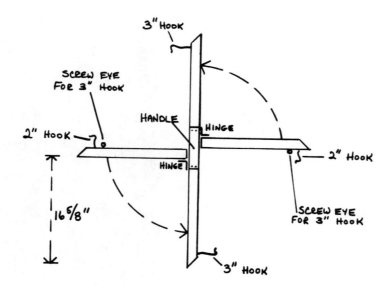

TABLE BASE — TOP VIEW

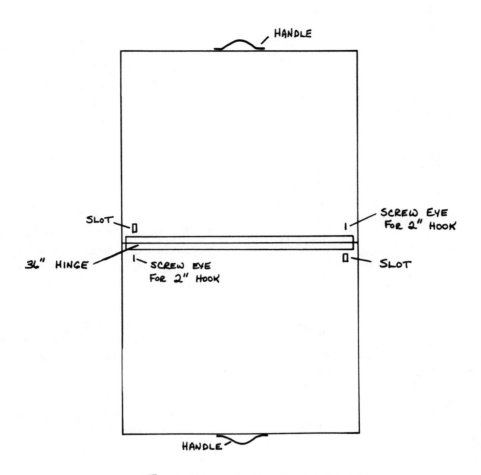

HANDLE

SLOT

SCREW EYE
FOR 2" HOOK

36" HINGE

SCREW EYE
FOR 2" HOOK

SLOT

HANDLE

TABLETOP — VIEW OF UNDERSIDE

—— trim large piece left from 30" door to 36" length, to be used as the base center

—— glue wood blocks in all open ends for reinforcement

—— clamp and dry overnight

—— to camouflage the appearance as a door, have millwork shop cut each of the reinforced ends of the table base (four cuts) at a 45-degree angle; do not trim in length, simply recut to shape reinforced ends of base only (an alternative which produces a more refined look is to cover the reinforced ends with veneer tape)

—— it is easiest to apply polyurethane varnish now; several thin layers provide better protection than two thick applications

—— place the two pieces of the folding top face down on a flat surface, with the reinforced ends meeting in the center

—— with the 36" piano hinge open flat, align it on the seam

—— secure two screws on each side of the hinge near the center, two more at the top, and two at the bottom; test for smooth folding and minimal gap, and correct if necessary before securing all screws in the hinge

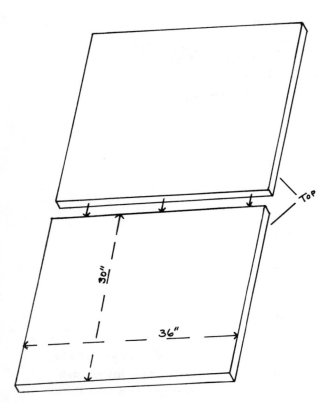

— in order for the top of the table to rest flat on the base, the handle with which you lift the base must be sunken, or mortised; mortise a slot in the center of the top edge of the base (if you have access to a band saw, you can cut a deeper, curved handle opening, but you must then cut the 30" hinges off slightly with a hacksaw so they will not overlap the hand space)

— the base wings should be positioned slightly off center so they will not interfere with the hinge of the folding top when the table is set up (refer to sketch for exact placement and direction before hinging the wings to the base center); with the base center on a flat surface, mark a line 16⅝" from the longer tip

— on that line, stand the flat end of one base wing and align a hinge in the right angle formed; again, with a few screws in the center, top, and bottom, test the swing and correct, if necessary, before completing the full line of screws

— — repeat with second hinge and second base wing on opposite side of the base center

— with the table base in its storage position, hooks and eyes will keep the base wings from flopping about as it is carried

— at each end of the base center, secure a 3" hook opposite each wing, near the end, and as close as possible to the top edge (see sketch)

— with the wings folded in, pull the hooks across both the base center and one adjacent wing, and mark a spot near

the top of the wing for the screw eye
— hooks in the base and corresponding eyes in the tabletop will stabilize the table while it's in use
— set the table up and center the top over the base
— from underneath the table, mark positions for hooks at each end of the base wings (now on the sides of the table); the hooks should be placed so they will be slightly taut for greatest stability
— mark corresponding positions for the screw eyes in the top

— the two screw eyes in the tabletop will prevent the top being closed flatly, so you must drill or mortise a small slit in the opposite side of the top for the eyes to sink into when the top is folded (see sketch)
— drill holes in the leather handles for four wood screws; use washers to relieve pull on leather
— position one handle in the top center of the base, which has been mortised; center the other two handles at each end of the tabletop; leave enough space to get a hand under the handles

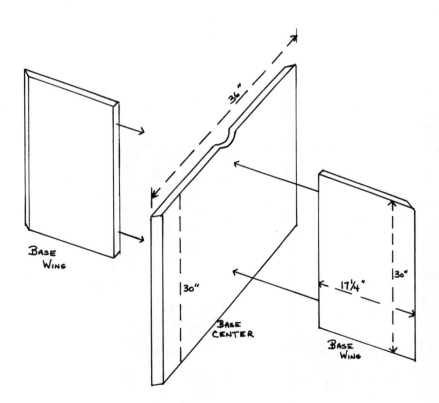

BASE
WING

36"

30"

BASE
CENTER

17¼"

30"

BASE
WING

The Very Highback Chair

Dennis Freedman

Cost $31 for two chairs Time: 6 hours

5¾" | 5¾"

EXTRA WOOD FOR CLAMPING BLOCKS

1'7"

11'5⁄8"

11'8⁄8"

11'5⁄8"

1 15⁄16"

Materials
(for a pair of chairs)

—— three 6'8" hollowcore doors, 1⅜" thick
—— 5' (5¼" nominal by 12" nominal) common pine shelving for fillers (your lumber store will furnish 1⅛" x 11½")
—— one quart primer
—— one quart black semigloss finish paint
—— tite bond glue by Franklin or Elmers professional carpenter's wood glue
—— fine and extra-fine sandpaper
—— six pieces shelving scrap for blocking when clamping

Tools

—— table saw (handsaw can be used)
—— router (1⅜" for joints)
—— vibrator sander (if needed to shave down fillers)
—— tape measure
—— six 2' adjustable planking clamps with pipe
—— 3" paintbrush

Method

Examine illustrations
—— cut hollowcore doors into four pieces as follows (see diag. #2):
Piece A (back): 60" x 14"
Piece B (seat): 13¾" x 14"
Piece C (shelf): 13⅛" x 14"
Piece D (leg): 15⅞" x 14"
—— cut pine shelving for fillers as per diagram #1
—— break down inner cardboard of hollowcore doors with a piece of scrap wood

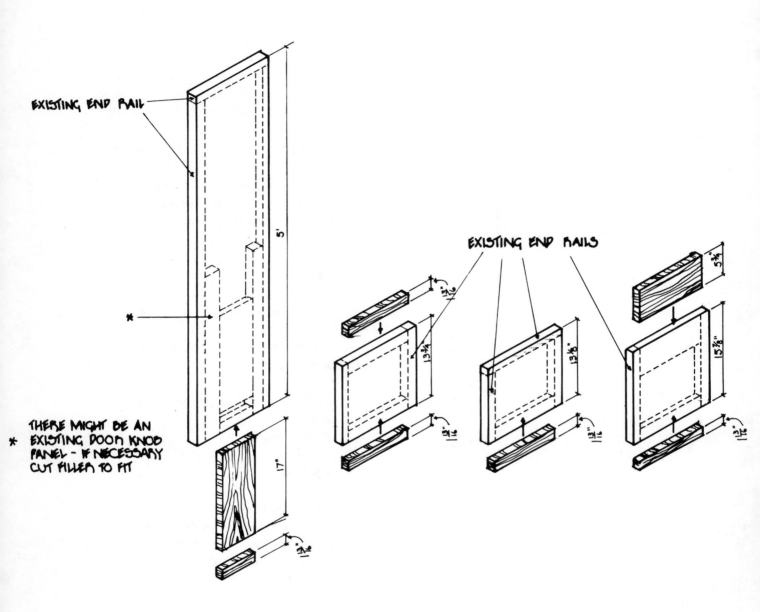

EXISTING END RAIL

*

* THERE MIGHT BE AN
EXISTING DOOR KNOB
PANEL – IF NECESSARY
CUT FILLER TO FIT

5'

17"

1 3/16"

EXISTING END RAILS

1 3/16"

13 3/4"

1 3/16"

13 1/8"

1 3/16"

5 3/4"

15 5/8"

2 1/4"

PIECE A
BACK

PIECE B
SEAT

PIECE C
SHELF

PIECE D
LEG

VERY HIGHBACK CHAIR

NNIS FREEDMAN

DIAGRAM #3

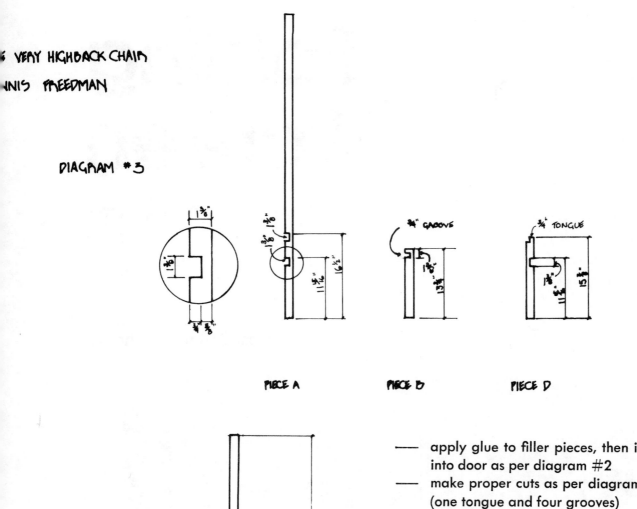

PIECE A   PIECE B   PIECE D

—— apply glue to filler pieces, then insert
     into door as per diagram #2
—— make proper cuts as per diagram #3
     (one tongue and four grooves)
—— sand with fine paper
—— apply glue to each of the joints and
     assemble as shown in diagram #4
—— clamp with wood blocking overnight
—— sand chair with extra-fine sandpaper
—— apply primer, then paint

Folding
Screen

Mark Nøre

Cost: $60 Time: 4 hours

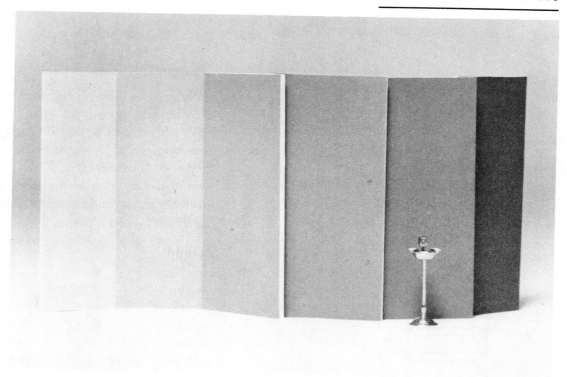

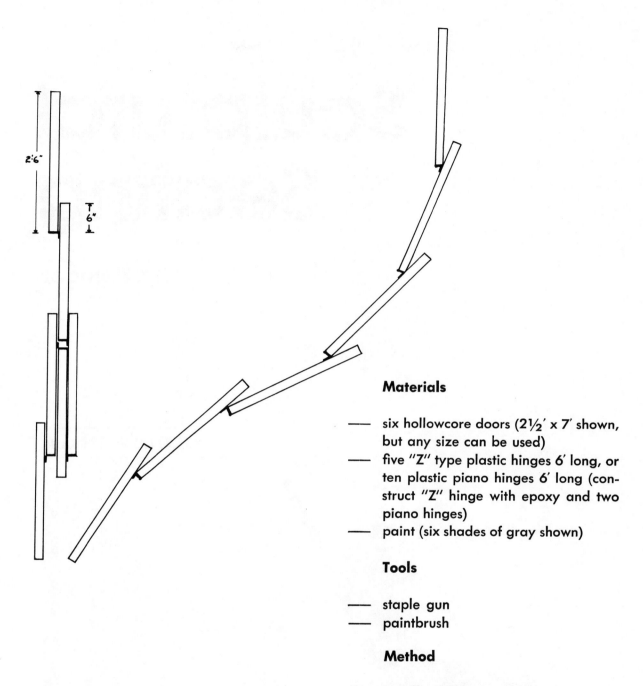

2'6"

6"

Materials

— six hollowcore doors (2½' x 7' shown, but any size can be used)
— five "Z" type plastic hinges 6' long, or ten plastic piano hinges 6' long (construct "Z" hinge with epoxy and two piano hinges)
— paint (six shades of gray shown)

Tools

— staple gun
— paintbrush

Method

Examine illustrations
— staple one end of "Z" hinge to one end of each door (five altogether)
— staple loose end of hinge at the 6" mark of each succeeding door (like arrangement shown) so that each door swings 180 degrees

Sculptural Seating

Gigi Hernaez

Cost: $30 Time: 11 hours

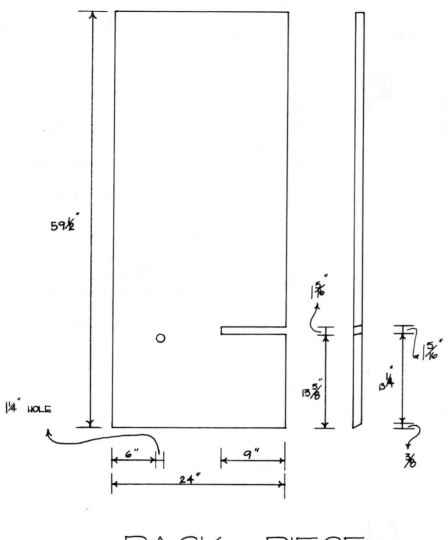

59½"

1 $\frac{5}{16}$"

13 $\frac{5}{8}$"

1 $\frac{5}{16}$"

1 $\frac{1}{4}$"

$\frac{3}{8}$

1 $\frac{1}{4}$" HOLE

6"

9"

24"

BACK PIECE

Materials

— two hollowcore doors, each 24" x 80"
— two 1¼" diameter wood dowels, 6" long
— 8' of 1" x 2", cut to 1" x 1⅛" wood as reinforcement

Tools

— paint
— sandpaper
— carpenter's glue

53

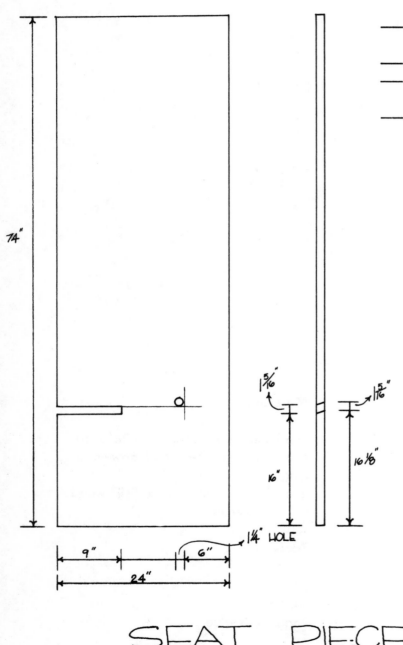

Method

Examine illustrations
— cut one door 59½" long for the back piece
— cut one door 74" long for the seat piece
— reinforce open ends with 1" x 1⅛" to fit inside the cut ends
— glue and clamp
— measure and cut slits at an angle; reinforce with 1⅛" wood
— to find the exact location of the hole, line up hole with the edge of the slits on both sides of the doors so that the dowels will go through at the same angle as the slits

74"

1 5/16"

1 5/16"

6"

16 1/8"

1¼" HOLE

9"

6"

24"

SEAT PIECE

54

FIG. A

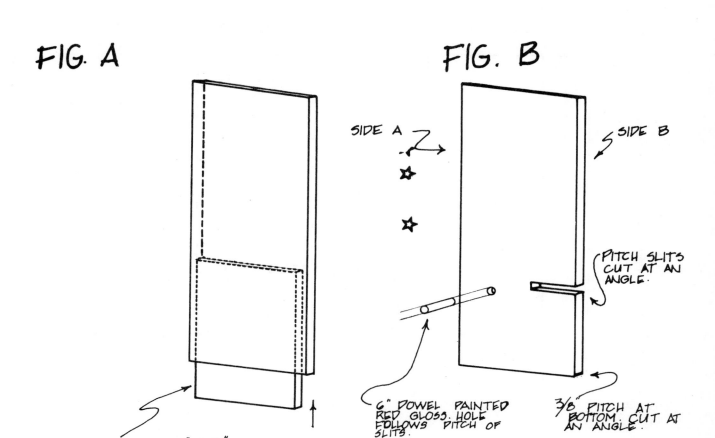

GLUED ¾" & ⅜" PLYWOOD

FIG. B

SIDE A

SIDE B

PITCH SLITS CUT AT AN ANGLE.

6" DOWEL PAINTED RED GLOSS. HOLE FOLLOWS PITCH OF SLITS.

⅜" PITCH AT BOTTOM. CUT AT AN ANGLE.

FIG. C

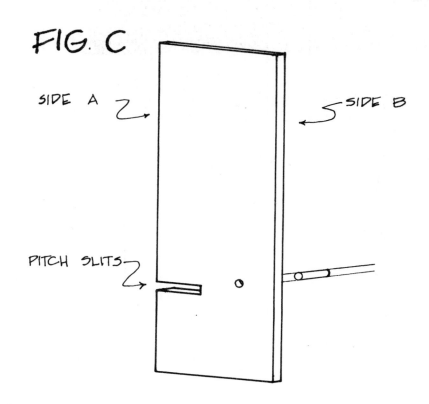

SIDE A

SIDE B

PITCH SLITS

SIDE A   SIDE B

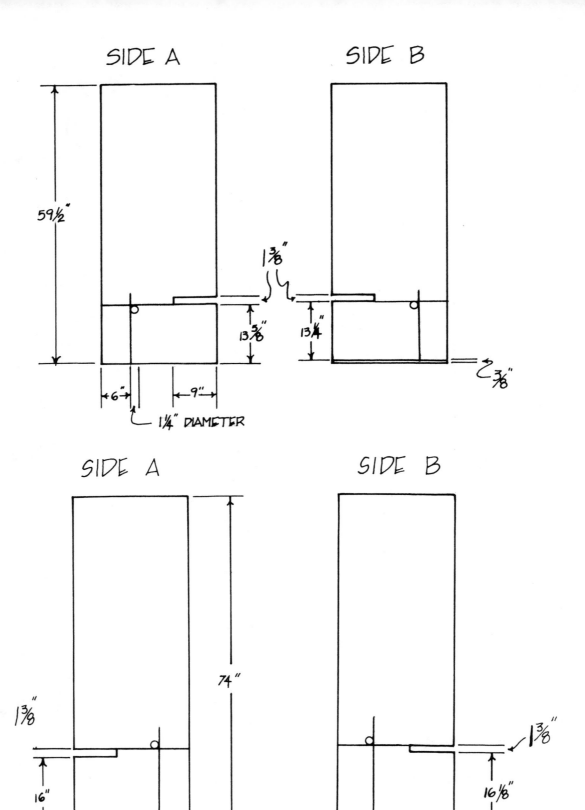

59½"

1⅜"

13⅜"

13¼"

⅜"

6"

9"

1¼" DIAMETER

SIDE A   SIDE B

74"

1⅜"

1⅜"

16"

16⅛"

9"

6"

56

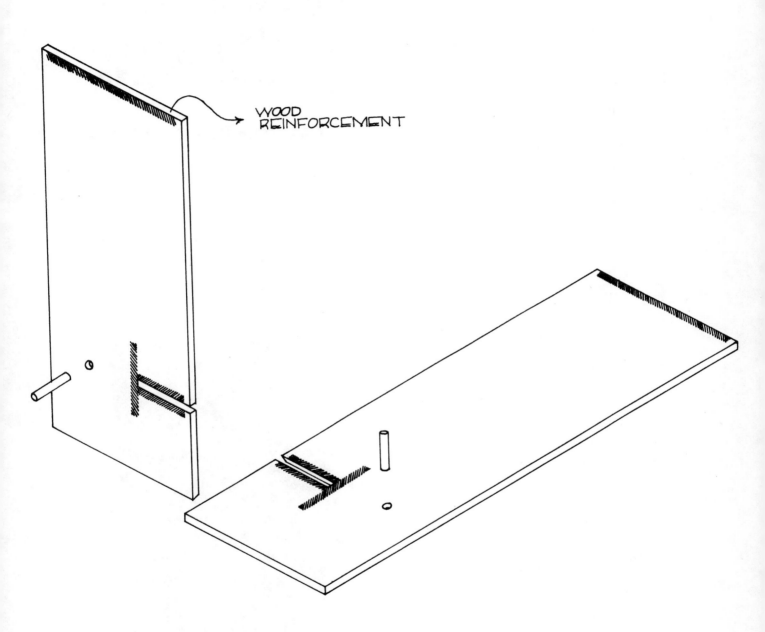

WOOD
REINFORCEMENT

Walnut Chair

George Thomopoulos

Cost: $17 Time: 15 hours

Materials

— one piece of walnut, 96″ x 34″ x ¾″
— wood screws, 1½″ and 1¼″

Tools

— electric saw
— crossaw
— screwdriver
— sandpaper

Method

Examine illustrations
— cut the piece into the eleven parts as shown (A through 12); sand each piece evenly
— examine diagram carefully, and mark the letters as per diagram
— then measure on parts A and B 110 degrees and on parts H1 and H2

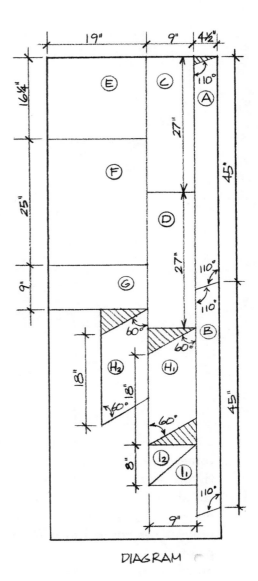

DIAGRAM

59

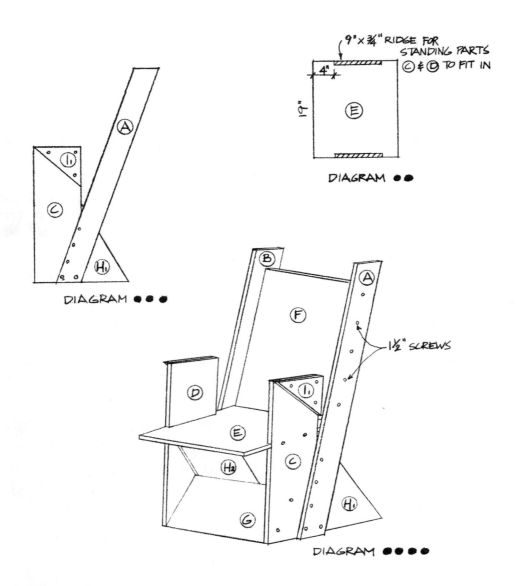

9" x ¾" RIDGE FOR STANDING PARTS ©&© TO FIT IN

4"

19"

E

DIAGRAM ●●

A

C

I₁

H₁

DIAGRAM ●●●

B

A

F

1½" SCREWS

D

I₁

E

C

H₂

G

H₁

DIAGRAM ●●●●

30 degrees on the outside smaller corner (the shaded parts on H1 and H2 are waste)

—— cut pieces I1 and I2 as shown (above diagram ●● shows how two grooves are formed in each side of piece E)

—— diagram ●●● indicates how the one side, which is made of parts C, I, A, and H1, is put together; exactly the same procedure will be used to form the other side with parts D, I2, B and H2.

—— the next step is the placement of E, the seat; place between the two sides

after measuring 16" off the floor

—— use 1½" screws to connect the seat with the sides

—— then take part F and put between parts A and B with one of its sides placed behind the seat

—— measure 2¼" on parts A and B from the edge facing the seat

—— hold part F in steady position, and with 1½" screws make a part of the already formed chair

—— final step: take piece G and place it between the legs of the chair in a position so that it forms a triangle with the floor

60

Needlepoint Sconce

by T. Shetchik

Cost: $10 Time: 1/2 hour

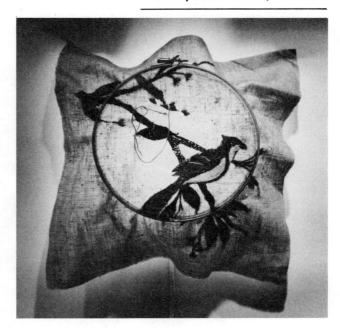

Materials

—— 4" deep cylinder of plexiglass
—— wire with socket, plug, and in-line switch
—— 7½ watt bulbs
—— needlepoint with outside hoop

Tools

—— drill
—— hook or nail

Method

Examine illustration
—— take plexiglass cylinder (diameter should be slightly less than that of needlepoint hoop) and drill a hole equally distant from both edges
—— feed wire through and attach socket and bulb
—— stretch needlepoint over cylinder and tighten hoop over outside edge

Laplander Chair

Mark Nøre

Cost: $16 Time: 8 hours

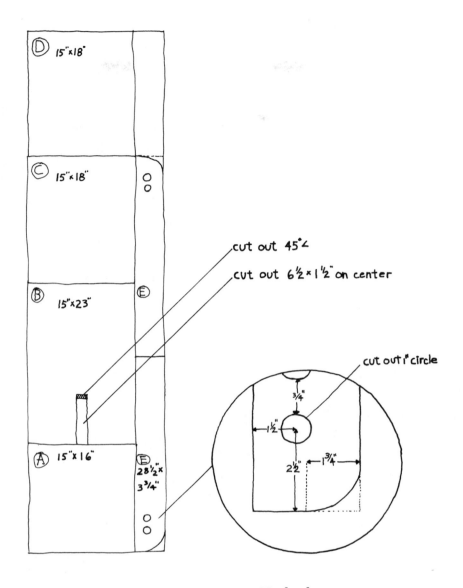

cut out 45°∠

cut out 6½" × 1½" on center

cut out 1" circle

Materials

—— ¾" plywood, 19" x 75"
—— four 4" wide "T" hinges
—— six strap hinges 4" wide
—— two 1" diameter dowels, each 6" long
—— one quart of paint

Tools

—— crosscut saw
—— drill with 1" boring bit
—— screwdriver
—— paintbrush

Method

Examine illustrations

—— cut plywood into lengths as shown in the cutout diagram: 15" x 18", 15" x 18", 15" x 23", 15" x 16", 3¾" x 28½", 3¾" x 28½"
—— cut out two 1" diameter circles on each piece E, located ¾" apart as shown in drawing
—— also cut a 1¾" radius curve on the bottom of piece E
—— lay out pieces A, B, C, D, and hinge

the basic zig-zag shape together (see exploded diagram)

— center the two back supports E on piece A, and then screw two sets of hinges for each piece A (you will want the two supports to be able to fold down flat to piece A when chair is dis-assembled)

For dining chair seat height (18"): add 4" length to Piece E, and shift place-ment of dowel holes up ¼" from original placement.

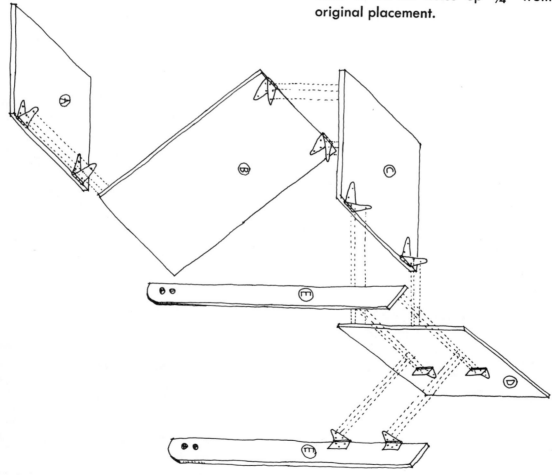

Laplander Table

Mark Nøre

Cost: $35 Time: 8 hours

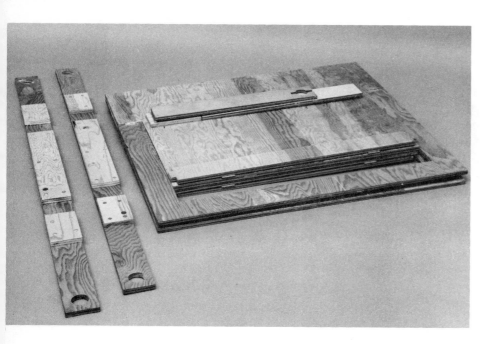

Materials

— one sheet ¾" plywood, 4' x 8'
— one sheet ¾" plywood, 12" x 71"
— four 4" strap hinges (¾" screws)
— eight 2" hinges (¾" screws)
— one 48" piano hinge

Tools

— circular saw
— handsaw
— screwdriver
— drill with 2" boring bit

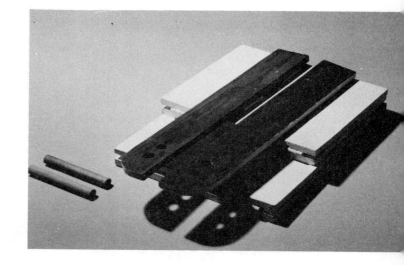

Method

Examine illustrations
— cut out plywood as shown in cutout diagram:
    A: initial cut 42" x 48" (two)
    B: cut "U" shape off of piece A 4" wide by 29" up the sides (two)
    C: 4" x 29" (see detail for cut) (two pieces)
    D: 4" x 28¼" (see detail for cut) (two)

    E: 4" x 4" (eight)
    F: 4" x 8¾" (two)
    G: 4" x 71" (see detail for 1" circle cut) (two)
    H: 4" x 40" (piece H is cut off of piece A) (cut away ¾" x 1" for notch)
— stack pieces A and screw a 48" piano hinge into the ends (this will enable the tabletop to fold together and protect it during storage)

66

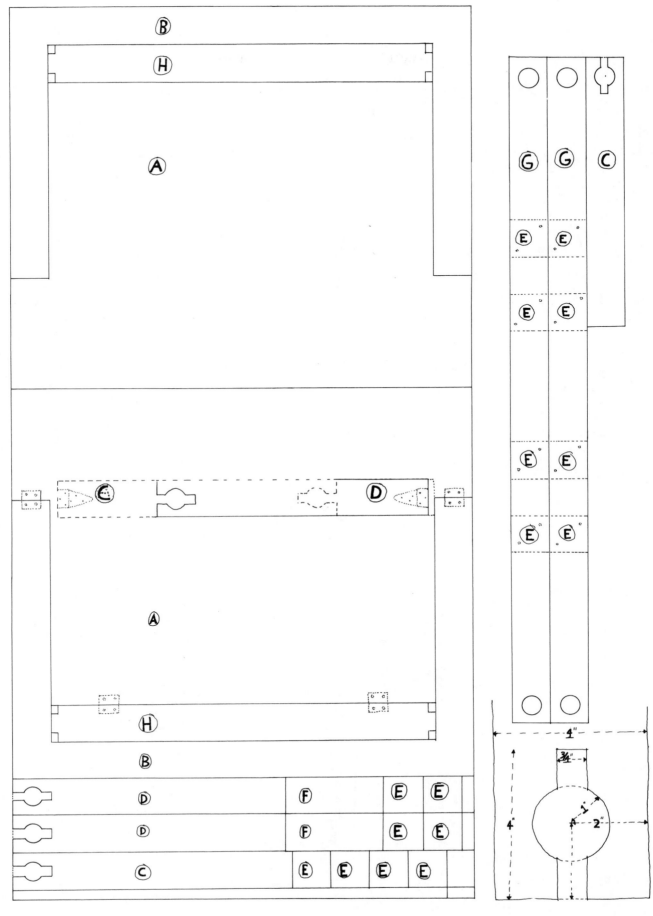

Details C, D, G

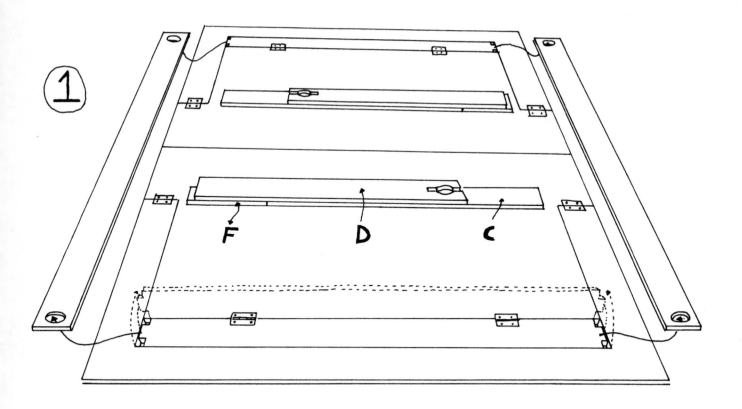

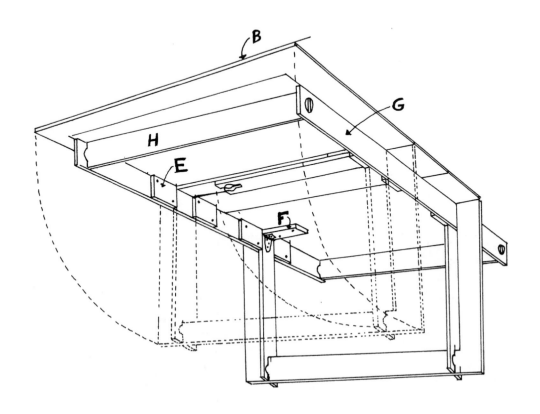

— fold out so tabletop will be down
— hinge piece B to piece A
— repeat for both sides
— lay pieces h in place and attach two hinges
— repeat for both sides
— using 4" strap hinges, screw piece C to piece A, allowing ¾" clearance for opening
— screw piece F to piece A (Fig. 1.)
— using 4" strap hinges, screw piece D to piece F, also allowing ¾" opening clearance
— use steps 4–6 for both sides

— cut out 1" circles on both ends of piece G (see 1" circle detail)
— measure in from the ends of piece G, draw a line at 21" and at 25"
— attach support pieces E at the 21" line and at the 25" line

Assemble

— raise pieces H 90 degrees and attach piece G in the notch
— raise piece B 90 degrees and slide piece D up into place and also piece C
— turn table over, and it's ready to go

Triangle Folding Chair

Sara Jo Stander

Cost: $40 Time: 15 hours

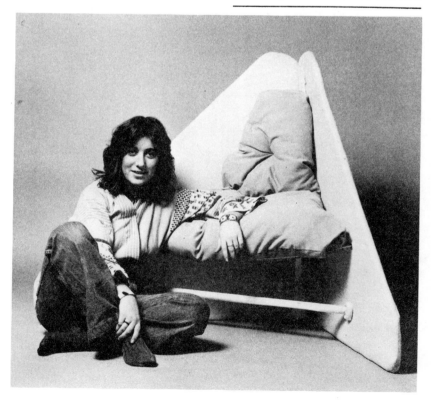

Materials

—— 4' x 4' square of plywood
—— 35" dowel, 1" diameter
—— four extra-large hinges, screws
—— eighty-four grommets and backs
—— 9 yds. plastic clothesline
—— two pieces muslin, each 4' x 4'
—— 2½ yds. 45" width material, for cushion
—— two bags polyester stuffing

Tools

—— drill
—— 1" bit, ⅜" bit
—— grommet setting tool
—— pins
—— tape measure
—— hammer
—— screwdriver
—— sewing machine, and someone who can sew
—— jigsaw or electric handsaw

Method

Examine illustrations
—— cut plywood square diagonally in half
—— placing both triangles exactly on top of one another, round the corners at about 42"
—— Follow diagram for marking location of holes; measure three points as shown: between points A and B, measure and mark eleven points, 1½" from each other (there should be a total of twenty-one points, including A, B, and C)
—— place triangles exactly on top of each

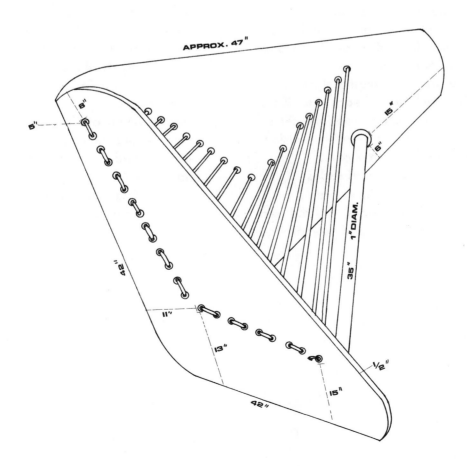

APPROX. 47"

71

other, and drill ⅜" holes at all points
—— from point C, measure over 15" and up 6" from the base, and mark the point
—— separate the triangles, and drill 1" diameter hole in each piece from the outside in a 45-degree angle
—— cut dowel at 45-degree angle on both ends
—— place both triangles on top of one muslin square; trace around pieces, then mark a 2½" seam allowance around outside of triangles
—— cut
—— do the same with other square of muslin
—— sew two pieces together, leaving the base side open
—— sew other two same way
—— turn to right side out
—— fit covers to make sure they're right, then remove and trim seams
—— place each cover on a triangle, and mark all holes with a pencil on both sides of both triangles
—— remove covers again and place grommets on each side of each side of the material (in other words—one set on the inside and outside of the outside)
—— do the same for other cover
—— place covers back on triangles
—— mark where dowel holes are
—— only on the inside sides, cut and fold under edges, and hand sew around

—— fold edges under at base of chair and hand sew shut
—— place triangles on floor, back edges touching
—— place, mark, and insert hinges (these will be on the inner part of the chair)
—— stand chair up and fit dowel
—— mark points where dowel fits holes
—— remove dowel, pin muslin, and mark around dowel
—— sew cover for dowel
—— replace in chair
—— string clothesline through holes back and forth, knotting at ends and leaving sufficient slack

Cushion
—— measure from top holes to bottom holes (should be about 45" long)
—— fold material in half, insides facing out
—— measure and mark length
—— measure width of inside of seat at various points and mark on material
—— connect points (the cushion should resemble a triangle), leave 3" seam allowance around
—— stitch cushion around, rounding corners and leaving about 5" unsewn
—— turn right side out and stuff
—— hand-sew remainder shut
—— tack stuffing down with a couple of stitches in top center of cushion
—— sit

Cube Lamp

by Gigi Hernaez

Cost: $10 Time: 1 hour

Materials

— cord-hung socket with bulb
— wire grid
— rice paper

Tools

— metal cutting shears
— scissors
— contact cement

Method

Examine illustration
— cut wire grid into an equal-sided cross
— fold so that grid forms a cube with open bottom
— cover outside of cube with rice paper, trim, and dab with glue
— feed wire through center of top and knot cord to hold in place

S.O.S.
Night Table

George Thomopoulos

Cost: $26 Time: 12 hours

Materials

— one piece of birch plywood, 96" x 48" x ¾"
— two light bulbs
— electric wire
— finishing nails
— glue
— sandpaper
— four casters
— hinge
— magnet
— screws
— plastic wood

Tools

— electric saw
— drill
— sander
— jigsaw
— hammer
— screwdriver

Method

Examine illustrations
— following diagram ● cut the plywood into ten pieces plus the base pieces

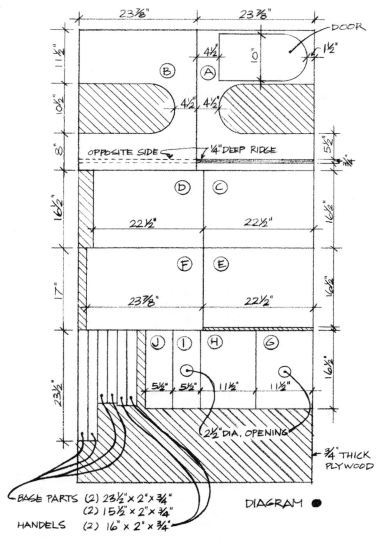

23⅞"   23⅞"

DOOR
11½"   4½"   0   1½"
B   A
10½"   4½" 4½"
OPPOSITE SIDE   ¼" DEEP RIDGE   5½"
8"   ¾"
16½"   D   C   16½"
22½"   22½"
17"   F   E   16½"
23⅞"   22½"
J I H G   16½"
23½"   5½" 5½" 11½" 11½"
2½" DIA. OPENING
¾" THICK PLYWOOD

BASE PARTS (2) 23½" x 2" x ¾"
(2) 15½" x 2" x ¾"
HANDELS (2) 16" x 2" x ¾"

DIAGRAM ●

——from piece A and B cut off shaded
parts

——also from piece G and I cut a 2½"
diameter circle in the middle of each
piece

——take piece A and put it opposite piece
B as shown at diagram ● ●

——take pieces H, I, J, G, and nail them at
the place indicated by broken line in
diagram ● ●

—— ● ● ● diagram shows how pieces
E,D and C,F sliding tray top is placed

——the two light fixtures are screwed on
piece E and C (behind the two holes
a small hole on E will let the electric
wire go through under the base; a

narrow ridge on the ¾" side of piece
B will lead the wire from the top light
fixture towards the floor): leave ¾"
all around from the bottom part

——according to the size of each side,
apply glue and nail the 15½" x 2"
x 23½" x 2" base parts

——on the underside of each corner, attach casters

——turn the whole unit right side up

For reading, slide the top piece F away
from the light and turn the light bulb on the
upright position.

For drawer light, close sliding door.

For a floor light, turn on the light in-
stalled on the base.

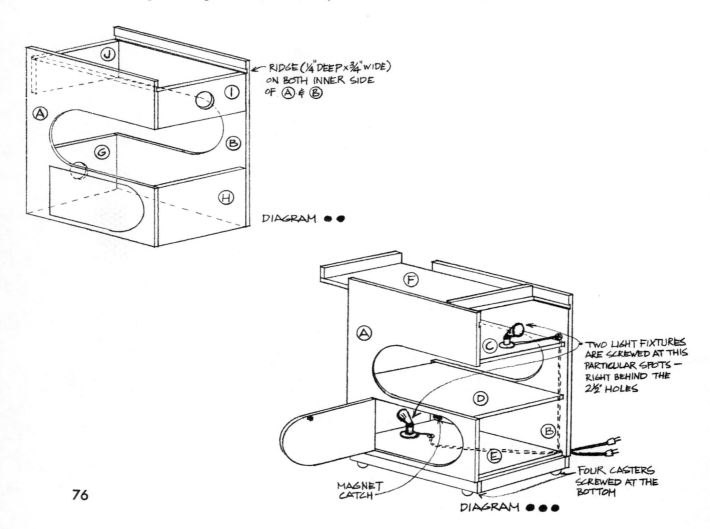

RIDGE (¼"DEEP x ¾" WIDE)
ON BOTH INNER SIDE
OF Ⓐ & Ⓑ

DIAGRAM ● ●

TWO LIGHT FIXTURES
ARE SCREWED AT THIS
PARTICULAR SPOTS —
RIGHT BEHIND THE
2½" HOLES

MAGNET
CATCH

FOUR CASTERS
SCREWED AT THE
BOTTOM

DIAGRAM ● ● ●

Canvas 1x2 Chair

John Kellas

Cost: $9 Time: 7 hours

Materials

— twelve carriage bolts, ¼" x 2½", with nuts to fit and washers
— 1" x 2" common pine sizes:
  Three 8" lengths
  One 6" length
  One 4" length
— 1½ yds. boat canvas
— white glue
— penetrating finish

Tools

— handsaw
— jigsaw
— electric drill
— sanding disc
— ¼" drill bit
— brace
— ¾" drill bit
— ⅞₆" wrench
— sandpaper, medium and fine

— sewing machine
— nylon thread
— old brush (for penetrating finish)

Method

Examine illustrations
— cut the 1" x 2"s into lengths shown in drawing #1
— drill ¾" holes in parts B and E as noted in drawing #2
— using the carriage bolts, assemble the 1" x 2"s into two chair sides (see drawing #3 for arrangement of parts); insert carriage bolts so that smooth heads are on outside of chair
— trim off the ends of the 1" x 2"s that are jutting out, except for the front of pieces E (see diagram #3)
— disassemble and smooth the edges and the corners of the 1" x 2"s with the sandpaper and disc sander
— cut dowels down to 23"

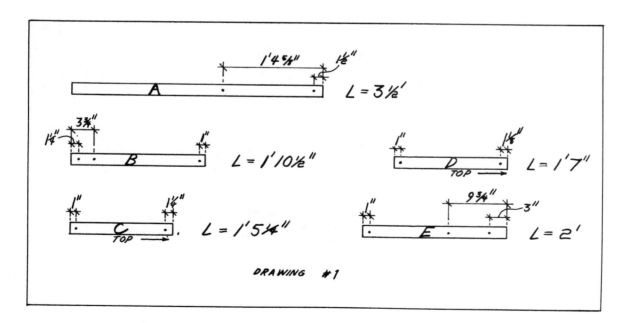

DRAWING #1

78

— glue pieces D together with two dowels, and pieces C together with the remaining two dowels
— apply penetrating finish to all wood pieces according to directions on can
— after finish is dry, assemble chair; leave off the nuts and the bolts that hold parts B together; remove the inner B's and lay them nearby
— for the seat, you will need a piece of canvas 36" x 3' 5¼" long
— in each long side of the canvas, cut a 3½" wide gap 16½" from one end (see diagram #5) (this smaller area of canvas is the seat area, while the larger will be the back area)
— trim ¾" off each side of the smaller area of canvas
— fold under edges on short ends 1½" and hem
— turn under sides 4½" and stitch across fabric 2¾" from fold; do this for both back area and seat area

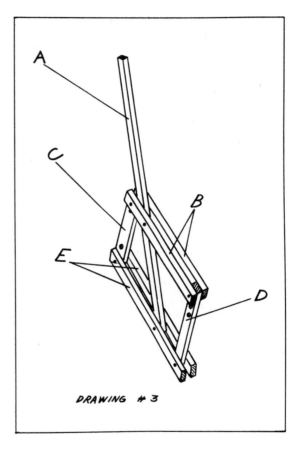

DRAWING # 3

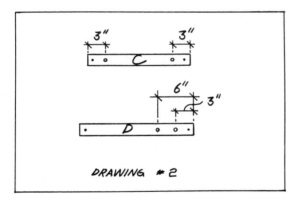

DRAWING # 2

— your canvas should look something like the bottom sketch in drawing #5 with four separate "sleeves"

— to assemble chair, slip the long sleeves down over the back supports (parts A)

— slip the two loose 1" x 2"s (part B) through the "seat" sleeves, put the 1" x 2"s onto the loose bolts, attach the nuts and washers and tighten; your chair is now completed

— to remove the canvas for washing reverse the last two steps

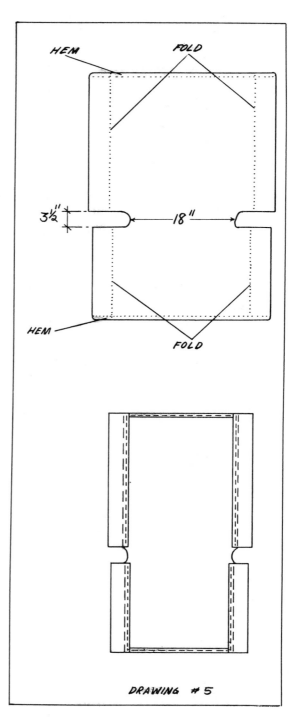

DRAWING #5

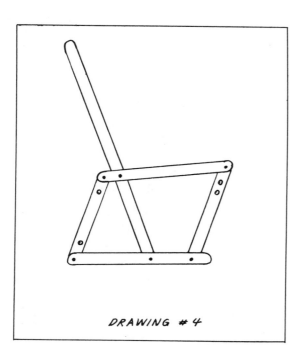

DRAWING #4

Optional

You could make your chair out of a hardwood, such as birch, if you wanted. This would make the chair stronger, but would be much harder to work with and much more expensive.

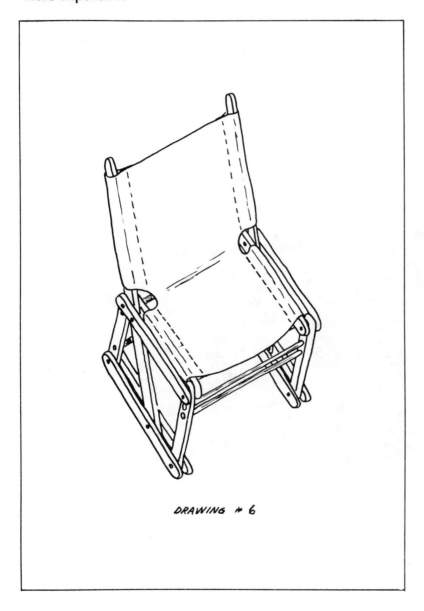

DRAWING # 6

Coffee Table

Sara Jo Stander

Cost: $22 Time: 9 hours

Materials

— one piece plywood or oak, 14½" x 30"
— 12′ 1″ x 8′ pine (buy clear pine if it's affordable, it saves time)
— two 31½" wooden dowels, ⅞" diameter
— latex enamel basecoat
— paint or stain

Tools

— table saw
— miter
— jigsaw
— drill press
— electric sander
— sandpaper
— glue
— clamps
— hammer
— 1½" finishing nails

Method

Examine illustrations
— cut all basic pieces; cut the 1 x 8 lengthwise so you have one piece 1¾" wide, and one piece 3¾" wide; put the 3¾" piece aside for later; it will eventually be used for the legs
— cut the 1¾" wide piece so that you have two pieces 31½" each, and two pieces 19" each (these will become the frame around the table top); miter the ends of these pieces at a 45-degree angle
— from the excess of that piece of wood, cut two pieces 17½" each in length, and four blocks 1¾" x 1½" (these are the support blocks)

— take the support blocks and glue one on top of each 17½" piece at both ends, making sure all edges are flush
— clamp until dry
— turn the plywood top upside down, and place the supports (#3) at either end so the top of the table is flush with the tops of the blocks; glue, and drive a nail through the bottom of each block
— clamp until dry
— when dry, turn the top right side up; glue the 19" framing pieces to either end of the table (keep the top flush); drive a nail or two from the frame into each block
— clamp until dry
— fit the other two pieces in place (31½") glue, nail, and clamp (there will be a space between these two pieces and the tabletop of about 1½"; that space is a track for the legs)

Legs

(Made from the 3¾" wide piece of wood, which you may have forgotten about already. Make sure you have every scrap until you're finished. I almost threw all the wrong pieces away!)

— cut eight pieces, each 15" long; at one end of each leg, measure up 4" and drill a ⅞" hole
— at the other end, measure over 1½" from each side; this should leave ¾" in the center, measure down 1¾" from the center
— cut out the rectangle with jigsaw
— place four legs on each dowel

To Assemble

—— just place the tabletop over the legs
so that the side frames fit into the cuts
you've made

That's it. It sounds kind of complicated, but
it took me longer to figure out how to write
these directions than it should take to make
the table.

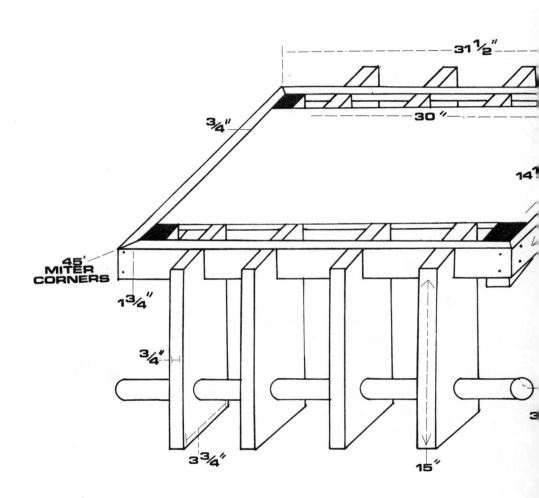

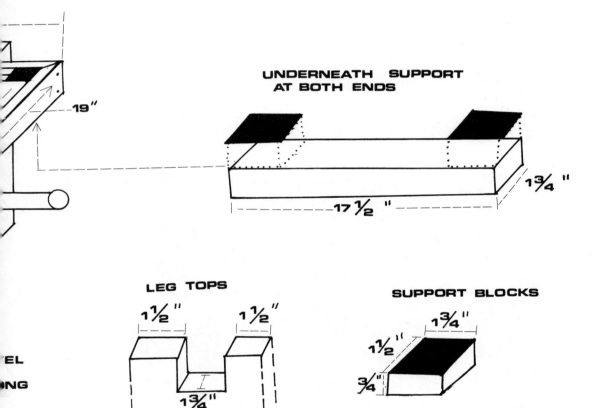

**UNDERNEATH SUPPORT
AT BOTH ENDS**

19"

17 ½ "

1¾ "

TEL

NG

LEG TOPS

1½ "   1½ "

1¾"

SUPPORT BLOCKS

1¾"

1½ "

¾"

85

Pillow Sofa

William Sarbello

Cost: $65 Time: 18 hours

Materials

Part letter	Name	Dimensions & Materials	Number of pieces
		¾" plywood	
A	arm rail	18" x 1"	4
B	arm rest	18" x 2¾"	2
C	leg	18" x 2"	2
D	lower leg assembly	5¼" x 2"	2
E	left and right rails	28" x 5"	2
F	center divider	28" x 4"	1
G	rail bottoms	27⅞" x 27⅞"	2
		¾" x ¾" pine	
H	blocks	4" long	6
J	bottom support blocks	12" long	8

Tools

—— screws: seventy-five 1¼" #6 flathead *sheet metal* screws, Phillips or slotted. Do not buy wood screws as they do not have enough thread to hold in the wood.

—— one 1" Stanley screw sink, part #1524A: This is a three-in-one drill bit. You should sink screws just below the surface of the wood. You are using 1¼" screws through 1½" of wood. If you sink the screws too far, they will come out the other side. You should be careful of this.

—— an electric drill: I suggest that if you do not have an electric screwdriver, you use your electric drill as one by buying a #2 Phillips head screwdriver bit and placing it in your drill. If you do this, you should be sure to buy Phillips-head screws.

—— 2 C-clamps: All pieces should be clamped securely in place and then the holes for the screws drilled and the screws screwed in tightly before the clamps are removed. Be sure to use blocks so as not to mar the wood.

This sofa is designed for two bottom pillows 32" square, overstuffed, at least 6" thick, and two back cushions 18" x 32", also 6" deep. The back rest is available in many different forms from most pillow shops. It's simply a rest normally used on the floor. Most any kind will work.

Note: There are two leg and arm assemblies. Assemble them both at the same time.

Method

Examine illustrations

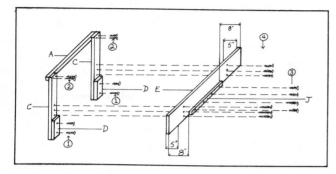

— attach part D to part C with two screws each
— attach part A to part C (these should be flush top and one side)
— attach part J to part E (this should be flush at the bottom and in 8" from either side)
— draw two reference lines 5" from each end
— now set this piece on top of part D (this will ensure that it is at the right height); now line the edge of part C up with this reference line; clamp, drill, and screw
— turn unit upside down

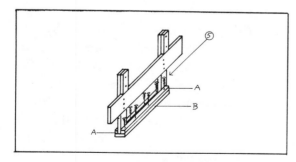

— attach part A to part B, making sure that it is flush on three sides

— attach another part A to part B flush on three sides; you are now finished with the leg assembly (it should be noted here that the last steps are mirror images of each other; that is, they are exactly opposite of each other)
— attach part H to each end of back rail (this piece should be positioned flush

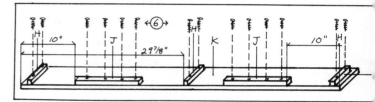

with the bottom, lined up with a reference line 10" from each edge)
— this is the tricky part: attach one part H flush with the bottom, lined up with a reference line $29\frac{7}{8}$" from the *left* edge as you face the bottom
— place a part H flush with the bottom, lined up with a reference line $1\frac{1}{8}$" from either edge
— place a part J flush with the bottom, lined up with a reference line 10" from either edge
— place a part H flush with the bottom, lined up with a reference line $29\frac{7}{8}$" from the *right* edge as you face the bottom (this part must be in the same position as its opposite piece or the bottoms will not fit in)

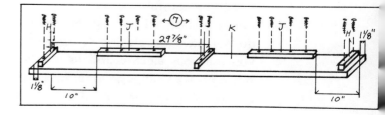

— attach a piece J flush with the bottom, lined up with a reference line 8″ from either edge

— place one of these on each side of piece F

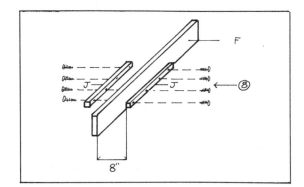

8″

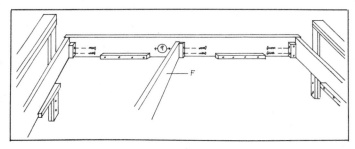

— attach part K to leg assemblies as shown (note that at this time the leg assemblies must also be exactly opposite; this is easily accomplished because these pieces are exactly symmetrical—simply face them so that the screw holes on each face inward)

— now attach part F to the 29⅞″ side of the middle block H on either side (this should make two 28″ squares; if they are not the same, you probably have attached part F to the wrong side of the blocks; change this now)

— measure in 1½″ from each edge of

part G; connect these lines with a diagonal line and cut off all the corners

— place bottoms into sofa (they should fit snugly; they will make the sofa square and strong)

— now place the back rests on the bottoms and place the cushions into their compartments

— now sit down and relax—you've earned it!

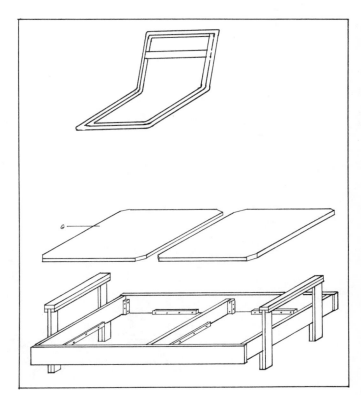

Table

William Sarbello

Cost: $35 Time: 10 hours

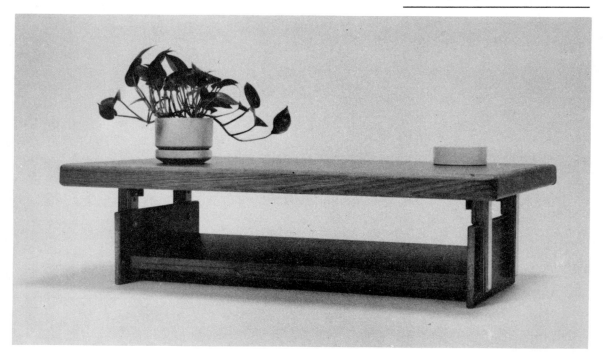

Materials

Part letter	Dimension	Name	Number of pieces	Material
B	38" long	top block	2	¾" x ¾" pine
C	20⅞" long	top block	2	" "
D	22½" long	top rail	2	1" x 2" pine
E	39½" long	top rail	2	" "
K	14" long	leg block	2	¾" x ¾" pine
L	5" long	shelf block	2	" "
A	38" x 22½"	top	1	¾" plywood
F	31" x 10"	shelf	1	" "
G	31" x 2"	shelf rails	2	" "
H	6" x 18"	shelf supports	2	" "
J	2" x 9"	legs	4	" "

Tools

—— screws: seventy-five 1¼" #6 flathead *sheet metal* screws, Phillips or slotted. Do not buy wood screws as they do not have enough thread to hold in the wood.

—— one 1" Stanley screw sink, part #1524A. This is a three-in-one drill bit. You should sink screws just below the surface of the wood. You are using 1¼" screws through 1½" wood. If you sink the screws too far, they will come out the other side. You should be careful of this.

—— an electric drill: I suggest that if you do not have an electric screwdriver, you use your electric drill as one by buying a #2 Phillips-head screwdriver bit and placing it in your drill. If you do this, you should be sure to buy Phillips-head screws.

—— two C-clamps: All pieces should be clamped securely in place and then the holes for the screws drilled and the screws screwed in tightly before the clamps are removed. Be sure to use blocks, so as not to mar the wood.

Method

Examine illustrations
—— attach part B to part A
—— attach part C to part A
—— attach part D to part C, making sure it is flush on both ends
—— attach part E to part B, making sure it is flush on both ends
—— attach part G to part F, being sure it is flush on three sides
—— attach part L to F, flush on one side, centered between two parts G
—— attach two of these

— attach two parts J to each part H (these should be 2″ from the bottom and 2″ from each side)
— attach part K to each of these parts J, flush on each end (you make two of these; as shown in the drawing, they are mirror images of each other; be sure to do it as shown in the drawing)
— draw a reference line on the bottom of the tabletop, 2″ in from part C; draw two of these, one on each end
— attach the shelf to the legs: center the

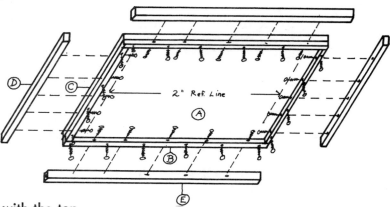

shelf assembly on part H with the top of the shelf 3″ from the bottom; attach this with two screws
— do this to both sides
— center this assembly on the bottom of the tabletop, part A, and line this up with the outside edges of all parts J with the 2″ reference line that you drew
— attach this to the top with screws
— turn the table right side up—it is now ready to finish and use.

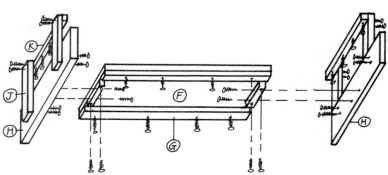

The Stuffed Shirt Lamp

Katherine Pearson

Cost: $20 Time: 1 hour, plus overnight drying

Materials

—— one white tuxedo shirt, any size, with black tie and studs and cufflinks (purchase used from tuxedo rental shop)
—— liquid fabric stiffener (one quart bottle) from craft and hobby shop
—— one porcelain electric socket for light bulb
—— wood base 6" x 6" x 1"
—— one white flat-wire
—— white electric cord 6' long
—— one white in-line switch
—— one oversized light bulb, 25 watt
—— heavy duty plastic, about two square yards
—— large oval-shaped balloon
—— two cardboard evening-dress forms, from a dry cleaner
—— masking tape

Tools

—— drill
—— screwdriver
—— deep broiler pan
—— oven rack

Method

Examine illustrations
—— wash and press shirt, if necessary, with heavy starch in collar and cuffs
—— build a makeshift mold from balloon to hold the shirt in shape until it dries; fold the cardboard evening-dress forms to make shoulders, and tape them tightly around the balloon for support
—— tape heavy plastic over this mold to prevent the cardboard from sticking

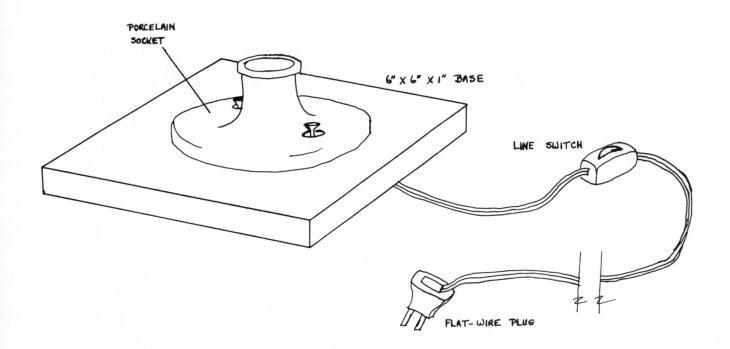

PORCELAIN SOCKET

6" X 6" X 1" BASE

LINE SWITCH

FLAT-WIRE PLUG

94

to the shirt; also spread heavy plastic over the table

—— saturate the shirt (except for the collar) with fabric stiffener (collar and cuffs look better if they are starched and are not dipped; the collar must remain flexible to insert the bow tie); you'll make fewer wrinkles in the shirt if you work with it flat in a large pan such as a deep broiling pan

—— shape the shirt over the balloon mold, working with the arms and shirttail to get a realistic but casual attitude; put the studs and cufflinks in

—— let dry overnight (much of the fabric stiffener will drip out of the shirt, so make sure the surface beneath is well protected)

—— the material that is tucked underneath will not dry overnight; on the second day place the shirt on an oven rack which has been evenly propped up to let air circulate beneath

Lamp

—— drill a hole through the center of the lamp base for the cord

—— center the porcelain socket on the base and screw it in place

—— connect the electric line to the two screws in the porcelain socket

—— attach the line switch about 18" from the base

—— attach the plug

—— when the shirt is completely dry, cut a hole in the bottom; break the balloon and remove the cardboard and plastic

—— slide the lamp base inside the shirt, and turn it on

Sod Boxes

by Dennis Freedman

Cost: $6 Time: 3 hours

Materials

—— one piece pine 1⅛" thick, 2" x 14"
—— one piece ⅛" plywood, 8½" x 11½"
—— Elmer's Glue
—— blue, white, black, acrylic paint
—— one brush
—— veneer brads

Tools

—— mat knife
—— plastic grass 8½" x 12½"
—— masking tape
—— miter corner clamp

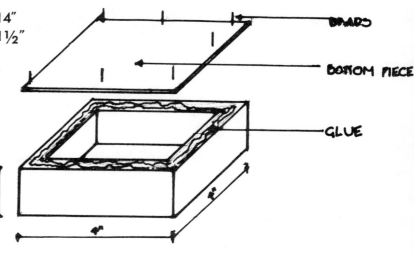

DIAGRAM #2

BRADS

BOTTOM PIECE

GLUE

DIAGRAM #1

Method

Examine illustrations
—— cut 1⅛" thick wood into twelve strips ⁵⁄₁₆" wide by 4" long, as in diagram #1
—— miter all edges at 45-degree angles
—— make three boxes by joining wood strips together; glue and nail, using a miter corner clamp to hold sides together when nailing
—— using ⅛" plywood, make three top pieces (4" x 4") and three bottom pieces (4" x 4")
—— as shown in diagram #2, glue and nail bottom pieces (4" x 4" plywood) to each of the boxes
—— cut plastic grass into three pieces 4" x 4" with a mat knife, and affix to each of the top pieces, using glue
—— using masking tape around the edges, paint cloudscape (refer to photograph) on the bottom of each box
—— your sod box is now complete

One-Armed Chair

by Tom Schefnick

Cost: $50 Time: 5 hours

Materials

—— three hollowcore doors, 6'8" x 2'6"
—— one 6" diameter cardboard circle
—— one 4' piece of wood, 1⅜" x ⅜"
—— one 7' long wood pole, 1⅜" diameter
—— 3 yds. upholstery fabric
—— 5" foam slab, 18" x 45"

Tools

—— table saw
—— saber saw
—— band saw

—— carpenter's glue and clamps
—— sandpaper
—— shellac
—— paint
—— foam cutting tool, or butter knife, ground sharp

Method

Examine illustrations
—— draw the first piece; measure all lines (except lines #5 and #7) from two points to make sure they are true
—— begin drawing piece A: draw line #1,

32" from the bottom of the door; draw line #2, 1" from the left side of door; draw lines #3 and #4; draw line #5 so that it measures 18" from where line #3 meets the edge of the door to where it crosses line #4; mark the spot where it crosses point #6

— cut a 6" circle out of a piece of cardboard, using a compass; place it in position X, tangent to line #1 with its center on line #2

— draw the curve

— draw line #7 tangent to this curve and passing through point #6

— draw the part of circle Y that connects lines #5 and #7

— draw most of circle Z to connect line #5 and the right edge of the door

— before cutting piece A, cut along the base of piece B with a table saw (this will assure a parallel cut)

— now cut out piece A (there is 1⅛" of wood structure around the edge of the door, so you may want to begin the curves with a saber saw; cut the rest of the way with a band saw)

— sand gently

— if there is more than the usual 1⅛" structure at the edges (usually doors have a bit more reinforcement where the knob will go), gently drill and chisel the extra wood out, leaving 1⅛" at the edge

— if the wood veneer separates from the structure, you can glue and clamp it later, but treat the veneer very gently

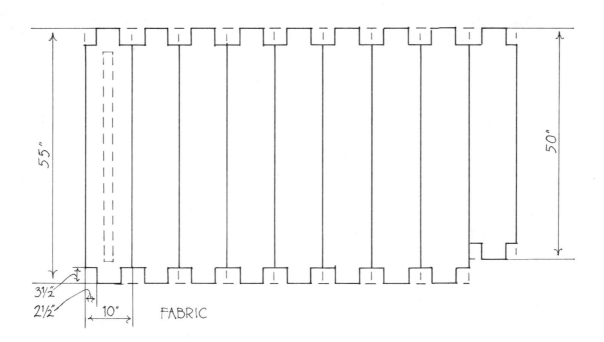

55"

50"

3½"

2½"

10"

FABRIC

100

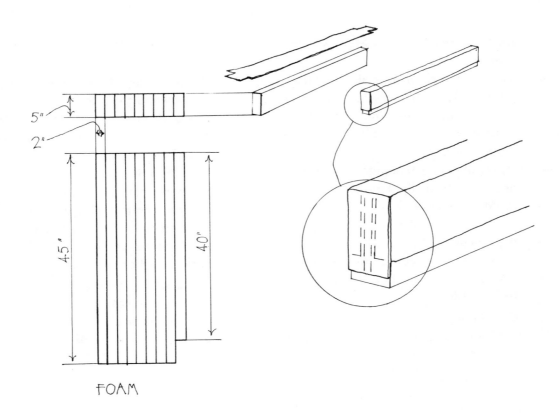

5"

2"

45"

40"

FOAM

— use piece A as a stencil; trace its curves to draw the other pieces; when you get to piece C, use it to make an arm

— draw line #1, the curve of circle X, and line #7

— now move the stencil up 9"; draw the curve of circle Z and line #5

— move the stencil down and to the left to continue line #5 and make the curve of circle Y meet line #7 (the "arm" will now be 24" from the base)

— cut out the rest of the pieces

— sand the curved edges of the veneer

— clear cardboard reinforcement away down to about 3½"

— stack the pieces and make sure their bases are aligned (leave out pieces A and C)

— clamp the pieces together

— draw the holes on the top piece of the stack (draw the holes on the insides only of pieces A and C, so that no holes will be visible from the outside of the chair)

— drill clear through (the drill will have a tendency to jump when hitting cardboard reinforcement); drill through the inside veneer only

— gently sand all the holes

— cut the twenty-four wood spacers as shown

— glue them on all the pieces except piece A as shown

— allow to dry

— apply shellac

— sand

— paint, two coats if needed

— stack all the pieces upright so they form the chair
— measure the chair from side to side
— subtract ¼", ⅛" for the veneer on each end piece (this will be the exact measurement of the poles; each pole should be 23⅜")
— try a pole in each hole to make sure it goes in with a slight resistance; sand slightly if necessary
— push and twist the poles through all the pieces
— glue on the two outside pieces
— clamp the entire chair from side to side, and let dry

Cushioning

— cut fabric as shown (the 50" piece is for the arm; the 40" piece is for the arm)
— cut a 5" slab of foam into nine strips as shown, using a foam cutting tool or sharpened butter knife (or have it cut)
— wrap the fabric over the top of the foam
— glue the sides and ends down
— while it's still wet, start at the front of the chair and stuff the fabric-covered foam into the hollow of the door; leave about 1½" of stuffing sticking out of the hollow
— allow a bit more stuffing for the curves, and make the foam really follow the curve of the chair
— allow cushioning to dry

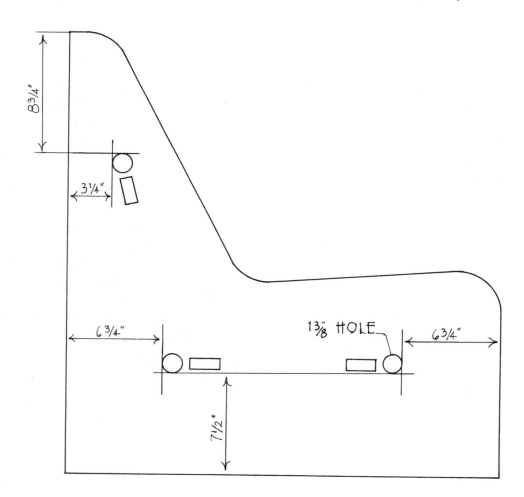

8¾"

3¼"

6¾"

1⅜" HOLE

6¾"

7½"

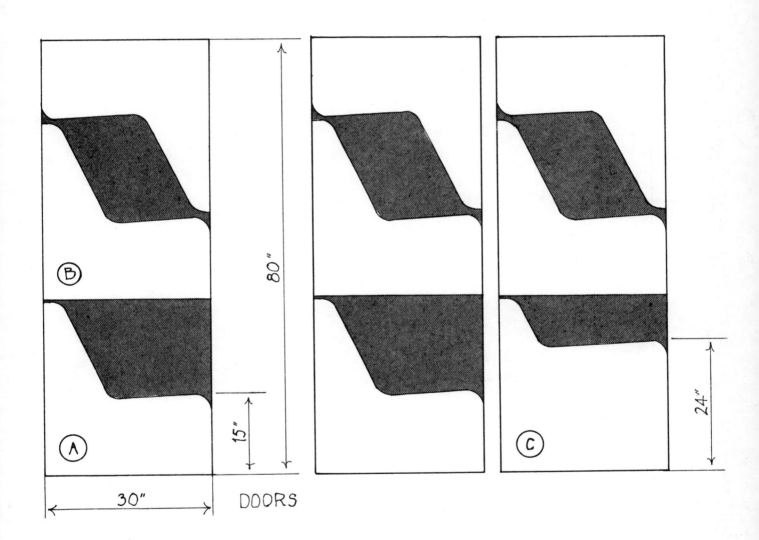

B

A

80"

15"

30"

DOORS

C

24"

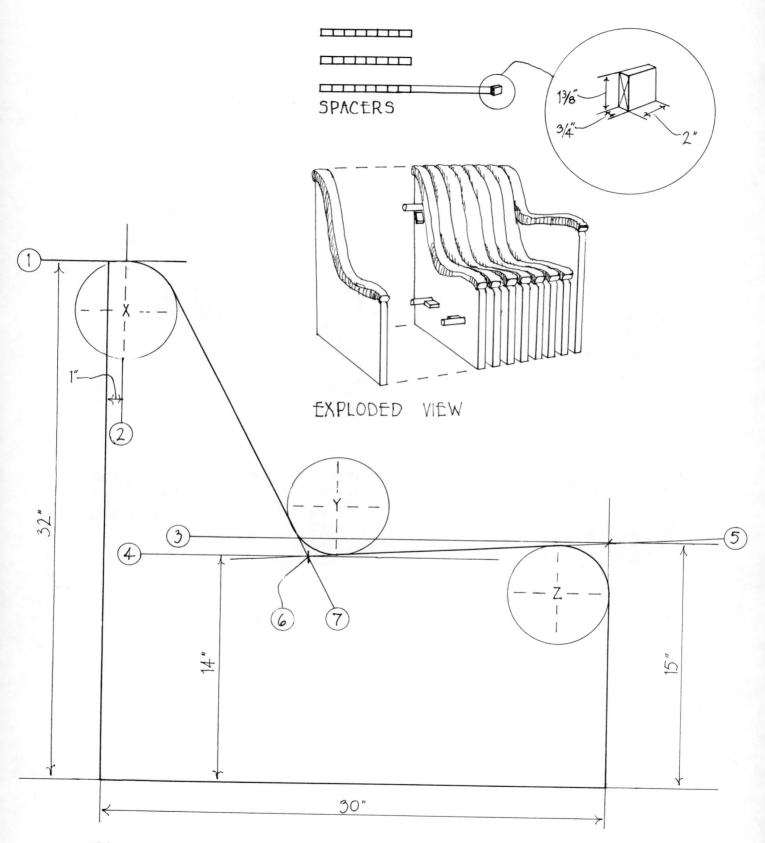

SPACERS

$1\frac{3}{8}"$

$\frac{3}{4}"$

$2"$

EXPLODED VIEW

1

X

1"

2

32"

3

Y

5

4

6

7

14"

Z

15"

30"

Entanglement

by Daniel J. Cohen

Cost: $2.95, cheap in
money, but the psychic
cost is incalculable
Time: 87 hours, plus time
spent cursing and kicking

Materials

—— pine or other rough-cut wood, 2′ x 4′, approximately 40′, or whatever's available (check out empty lots, wrecked houses)

—— two hinges, 3″ width

—— several hooks, various sizes

—— plastic clothesline, total length of 100′

—— four casters, if you want mobility

Tools

—— electric drill, or strong friends

—— ⅜″ drill bit

—— hammer

—— nails

—— screwdriver

Method

Examine illustrations

—— cut wood to approximate lengths and proportions: two main lower side bars; four bottom end pieces; two upper front side pieces; two upper back side pieces; two side pieces; two upper front pieces (remember to keep both sides symmetrical if possible; if not, enjoy the charm of uneven arrangements)

—— check to see if there really seem to be enough pieces of wood; that list didn't sound right to me

—— hinge together front and back pieces, matching, if possible

—— nail together the side and front pieces

—— nail together the top pieces

—— nail together the bottom pieces

—— nail together any leftover pieces, to be safe

—— after all nails are firmly in, see if it looks right; if not, rip out all nails

— try again
— when it looks all firmly nailed together, see if the hinges work to collapse it for easy storage in today's limited living space; if not, rip off hinges
— test new nails and hinges
— leave it the way it is, anyway
— drill holes for stringing clothesline: use drill bit (or borrow one from a friend; he won't mind what happens to it) and drill holes straight through wood from one side to another, if possible
— drill twenty-four holes on one side and more or less the same on the other; try to make them kind of opposite one another; to help you in this, take a cord and pencil, attach cord by staple to end of one beam, cut cord to length of distance between holes (easily found by dividing *exact* length of beam by 28.9 ((days in February some years))), then bring pencil out to total length of cord, make tiny mark with dark pencil on dark wood or light pencil on light wood (don't want to mar the beauty of your finished product), then pull cord out by trying to remove staple with thin screwdriver (best to borrow one from a friend, he won't mind), then repeat process down whole length of beam; repeat whole process on other beam; take out cord and pencil; and try to find the marks, just try
— when holes are all drilled, check to see if they align properly; if holes don't align, forget it
— string your clothesline; if you haven't been able to find a whole piece 100′ long, use several little pieces, knotted together; strong knots add that rough country look, but little tiny knots with bows in them have a tendency to come apart at unexpected moments, like when your mother is visiting, adding a delightful air of spontaneity
— thread the line carefully and precisely through the holes; if you have trouble getting the larger knots through the holes, drill a larger hole, trying not to cut the line as you drill; or undo the knots and retie them immediately, repeating process with each hole
—— when line is completely threaded through, anchor at each end by making a big knot, the real bulgy kind
— attach hooks and screw eyes wherever needed to hold it together (lines can also be attached to walls and ceiling, but that's cheating)
— varnish carefully, with fifteen to twenty coats; don't bother to wait for them to dry, just put on more; you can always paint it later
— if you don't like the clothesline color, paint it; but don't get a drop of paint on the wood
— if you don't like the wood color, paint it; but don't get a drop of paint on the clothesline
— clean up the mess, throw out the ruined nails and hinges, discard extra clothesline about to strangle your dog and any splintered wood not already in the bottom of your foot, repaint floor to cover blotches, stains, gashes, etc., and try to explain to your friend what happened to his tools
— enjoy the pride of handicraft life

Freebies,

(in 24 Minutes)
or No-Excuse Projects

This book is meant to be more than a collection of how-to instructions, a list of recipes for building specific pieces. The design projects were selected to try to illustrate an *approach* to furniture, and to making an environment for you and your friends to use and enjoy. What's important is the attitude, the values that inform these designs. The same values that I try to encourage in my students can also be expressed in commercial design work or in finding ready-mades.

In May of 1978, I introduced a new line of cardboard furniture at the Cooper Hewitt Museum of American Design, a branch of the Smithsonian Institute in New York City. It represents an attempt to offer inexpensive furniture and lighting that is still elegant, strong, and durable. Above all, it's an attempt to combat the incredible rise in the cost of materials and labor that has made factory-made furniture the enormously expensive white elephant it is today.

The basic cardboard material is actually thick brown (recycled) paper, strong yet inexpensive. The lounge chair shown here, for example, is made up of five pieces of cardboard that are glued together. Five wood strips are then glued to the base and one to the rear section to allow for stapling on the foam cushion and fabric. The honeycomb cardboard is constructed much like a beehive and is enormously strong. I was struck by its potential for furniture when I saw movers using cardboard pallets to lift heavy boxes in and out of trucks. (Pallets are platforms that shippers stack many cartons on and then use fork lifts to move about.) I figured that if this material could support such enormous weights, it could cer-

tainly support a human body. When this furniture is available commercially, it will be extremely sturdy; yet because it will be sold in parts, pre-cut at the factory, to be assembled at home with Elmer's Glue, it will also be very inexpensive.

I saw cardboard and noticed how it might be used for designing furniture. You can look around and see things that no one had yet thought to use for furnishing. Style at whatever price comes from pure delight in form and material, plus a little wit and spunk. Everyone can have it because everyone is creative—it's less a matter of tools and plans than of *seeing,* noticing an everyday object or possibility that no one else has noticed before. Smile at something; it may wink back. Just looking around you can be the best labor- and money-saving device of all. Good design doesn't mean making a lifetime investment, as they say in the ads. Do you really want to mortgage your future to your furniture?

Here are some examples of what I call no-excuse projects, because they're so simple that you can do them even if you can't slice cheese or tie your shoelaces. No instructions because you won't need them; these are really ideas that were just looking for someone to occur to.

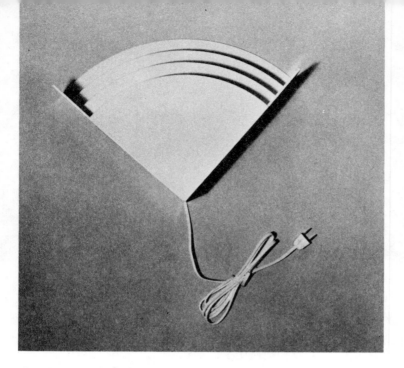

Art Deco Lighting Sconce

Here's a terrific light fixture. Believe it or not, it's really a record album holder. It's made of plastic and available in a number of beautiful colors for under $6.00 (made by Crayonne in France). A small 15-watt bulb and socket have been attached to the lower back. I used them myself to light a restaurant.

Up Light Alternative

You can save $25 while stylishly brightening a corner by using a twelve-inch aluminum tube from a plumbing and heating supplier. Just add wire, bulb, and a white porcelain socket.

110

Koolie Light

There are lots of wonderful wicker items available now at very low cost. From small trash baskets to hats like this one, they too make handsome light fixtures. Just string a wire and socket through the top.

Recycleable Records

Here the supplier is you. Admit that record is just taking up space; you'll never play it again because it was a mistake in the first place. Putting it in your oven for 2 minutes at 360° will get you a very limp piece of plastic. Shape it over a large orange juice can. The hole is already there for the socket and wire, and you have a hanging light fixture. Or invert for a cookie dish and fill it up.

Practical Kitchen Wall Decoration

The texture and warm neutral tone of wicker also make it a perfect wall decoration for many kitchens. Here are four roll baskets hung with four salad forks; they add welcome and definition to a bare spot and are also available for use. $4—or you may own them already.

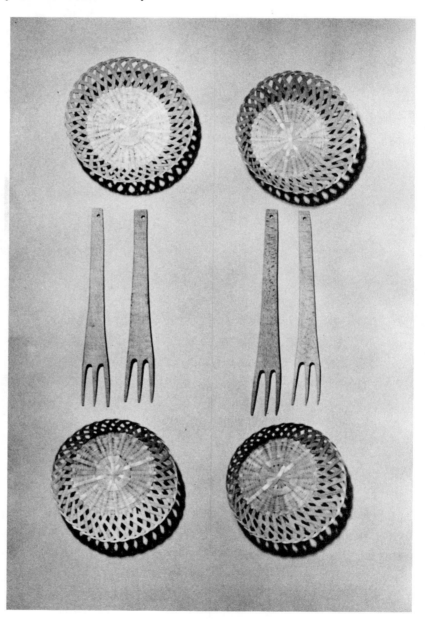

Instant Rolling Art

Or, hang your own view. Remember the rollers above the blackboard in school, where the U.S., Africa, or ancient Mesopotamia came and went? Now, with a shade, you can mount the weather or the time of day, to be pulled down at will and put away just as fast. Of course you can cover a window this way, too. If you hate to see the evening sun go down, it can be dawn or midnight whenever you like.

Bag Art

You must own some shopping bags. Take a look at them: more and more they're getting bold, brash, and gorgeous. Hanging them in striking arrangements makes just as much sense as hanging a poster—except the bags come with their own picture wire.

A Floral Deco Sconce

This sconce is actually a wall-hung ash urn that is available through office supply companies. Get it used, if possible, for better detail. Inside is floral styrene; adhesive and silk flowers bloom out the top.

Recycling the Drys

More flowers, this time dry ones you may have around the house. The day comes when they begin collecting dust and looking very drab. Try spraying them with high gloss paint. Instant spring.

116

Glitzing Strips

If you have a pipe protruding into a room or an old frame that could use a fresh look, try covering it with mirror-looking aluminum tape. One side is adhesive, the other looks like poured chrome. It's as simple to use as cellophane tape; just unroll and apply to the pipe or to a ceiling molding. It's so thin it goes on like gold leaf. Add a little glitz to your life.

I could go on and on—and so can you. And that's the point. This sort of design-by-find is a matter of opening your eyes. If you glance around you at this moment, you'll probably see an inventive, inexpensive idea for making your home more beautiful, more comfortable, or more fun. It's time now for you to stop reading and look up. . . . Enjoy!